Women of Color
COOKBOOK

RECIPES FOR YOUR HEART AND SOUL

Edited by Stephanie Moore

NIA PUBLISHING
Atlanta, GA

For my mother,

Shirley Roundtree Perry

You're the best cook I know. Thanks for putting together well balanced
meals, the best sweets and love into everything you fix. I've grown to
become a strong and humbled woman because of your food I took in.

Women of Color Cookbook
© 2003 by Nia Publishing

All scriptures quotes, unless otherwise indicated, are from the Authorized King James Version of the Bible

NIA PUBLISHING is an African-American owned company based in Atlanta, GA. Started in 1993 by Mel Banks, Jr., former marketing director or Urban Ministries, Inc., its first product was *The Children of Color Bible*. Nia has recently produced the *Wisdom and Grace Bible for Young Woman of Color* and the *Men of Color Study Bible*. The ownership, employees, and products of Nia Publishing are dedicated and committed to the cultural and spiritual growth of people of color, as individuals in the community and in the church. Nia can be visited on the internet as **www.niapublishing.com**

ISBN 0-529-11578-6

Published in cooperation with:
World Bible Publishers, Inc.
Iowa Falls, IA 50126
U.S.A.

Manufactured in the United States of America

1 2 3 4 5 6 7 8 CHG 08 07 06 05 04 03

Table of Contents

Articles

1 dream
1 map of a plan
1 heap full of effort
1 ounce of faith

Simmer on high until the dream is realized.

A Lesson in the Kitchen

One day Tammy was sitting at home with nothing to do so she thought she would bake a cake. Tammy had always been considered a good cook and her baking was excellent. She had gotten a cake recipe from a one of her worldly friends for a cake called a Heavenly Cake. The recipe was very different and Tammy had everything that the recipe called for so she thought she would try to bake this cake.

Tammy gathered all of the ingredients that the recipe called for and began to mix up the cake batter. She was so excited about this cake because she was one of the first to try it. She stirred up the batter until it was nice and fluffy, and then she proudly poured it in her baking pan. Just like many cooks, Tammy licked the bowl and the spoon and thought to herself, "This is going to be sooo good!"

She put the cake in the oven and let it bake for 40 minutes, just like the recipe told her to do. After the time was up, Tammy went to the oven and opened it, only to be disappointed. She looked at the cake and screamed out loud, "Oh no, what happened! I did everything I was supposed to do but my cake did not rise! I don't believe this—I always make excellent cakes!"

After taking a moment to calm down, she thought to herself, "I'll just spread some of God's Blessing flavored icing on the top—that should at least make it look good." Carefully, Tammy spread the icing all over the cake and she was right, it did look really good, but Tammy still was not satisfied. She thought, "Well, let me call my Christian friend, Stacey. She, too, is an excellent cook. Maybe she can tell me what I did wrong."

She called Stacey and told her about this cake, and told her that although she had all the right ingredients and did everything the recipe told her to do, the cake did not rise. Stacey quickly asked Tammy, "What were the ingredients of the cake?" Tammy told her:

1 cup gold
½ cup diamonds
¾ teaspoon money
⅔ cup jealousy
1 cup unforgiveness
2 cups pride

continued on pg. 6

continued from pg. 5

Tammy told her that she had mixed all the ingredients together and baked it at 350 degrees for 40 minutes. After realizing that the cake did not rise, she spread some of God's Blessing flavored icing over the cake to cover up what was underneath.

"Tammy," Stacey responded, "You can't make a HEAVENLY CAKE out of worldly possessions and spoiled fruit. You had nice worldly possessions, which is okay, but you mixed them with spoiled fruit, and then tried to cover it up with the God's Blessed icing. You didn't even have God in the mix. If you had put him in the mix, you would have quickly realized that the spoiled fruit—jealousy, unforgiveness, and pride—would never have helped the cake rise. If God is not in the mix of any and everything you do, just like your cake, it will not rise."

"Ohhh," Tammy said. "Now I understand. I had all of the worldly possessions and bad fruit, which is what the recipe called for, but I didn't have the main ingredient in the mix—God. Without God, my worldly possessions and spoiled fruit will not do me any good. Now that I think about it, what I really had was the ingredients for failure and there's nothing 'heavenly' about that."

Before hanging up the phone Tammy said, "Thanks Stacey. I'm so glad I called you. I have really learned a lesson in the kitchen today. Now I'm going to bake always with God in the mix of everything I make."

Jessica H. Love

Moral: You can do nothing successfully without God.

Microwave Cooking

For this writer, the microwave oven is one of the best kitchen/cooking inventions to come along yet. If I had to do without a kitchen appliance the microwave oven would be almost last or not even on my list. I remember in the early 60's when microwave ovens started to appear on the market, there were many skeptics. People feared that eating food prepared in a microwave oven would cause one to be filled with radioactive substances. Of course it was far from the truth, but changing the perception that people had was a difficult task.

Think of how things have changed! I often remind people that when I learned to cook, I did so on an old wood burning stove. When my children learned to cook, they did so by using the microwave oven. In fact, they bypassed the conventional gas and electric ranges all together! Today's microwave ovens have come a long way from their early predecessors. Not only are they sleek in apperance, but they also take up very little counter space and come in a variety of colors, shapes, and styles. Many models are programmed with a variety of foods that may be prepared in them. For example, if you are cooking fresh vegetables, you can touch a keypad until the type of vegetable you are preparing pops up on the screen, then you may be prompted to indicate the size and amount of the item. The microwave oven then proceeds to cook the vegetable for a preset amount of time.

Why do I prefer the microwave method of preparing foods? Foods cooked in the microwave oven are safe to eat. Foods retain their natural color, nutrients, texture, and shape very well because the foods do not have to cook as long as you would cook them using a conventional methods. Cooking foods in the microwave oven saves energy because of less cooking time. In the summer it keeps the kitchen cooler, again because of less cooking time, and because only the food gets hot—the microwave doesn't radiate heat into the entire kitchen like a traditional range. Using the microwave makes for easier cleanup. You can use paper products to cook on or in. One of my favorite ways to cook bacon in the microwave is to line a heavy-duty paper plate or regular with white paper towels, place the bacon slices on top, and cover with another sheet of paper towel. Wax paper and heavy-duty plastic wrap do very well in the microwave oven. Of course, if I am cooking rice, grits, scrambled eggs, baked apples, or meatloaf, I will use the appropriate microwave cookware. Pyrex is excellent in the microwave. In fact metal and wood are the only two materials not recommended for microwave use.

So you see, the microwave oven should be used for much more that popping popcorn, heating water for hot beverages, reheating, and defrosting. Be sure to read the manufacturer's instructions and/or cookbook that come with your microwave oven.

Go for it. It is a safe way to teach young children to prepare their own foods. Always remember safety, because the hot food that has been cooked in the microwave can burn one. May your microwave meals be fast, but good.

Shirley R. Perry, Family & Consumer Science Instructor

7

Microwave Tips

Bacon:

Put the bacon on a microwave safe rack or lined plate. Cover bacon with wax paper or paper towel. Cooking power should be at 100%. Cooking time for 2 slices is 1 to 2 minutes, for 4 slices is 2 to 3 minutes, and 6 slices is 4 to 5 minutes.

Butter:

For melting, place butter in an uncovered bowl on 100% power. Melting time for 2 tablespoons is 35 to 45 seconds, for ¼ cup is 45 to 60 seconds, and for ½ cup is 60 to 80 seconds. For softening, put butter in an uncovered bowl on 10% power. Softening time for 2 tablespoons is 40 to 50 seconds, for ¼ cup is 50 to 60 seconds, and for ½ cup is 60 to 70 seconds.

Chicken:

Season boneless, skinless chicken breasts to taste. Place chicken in a deep baking dish. Cover with plastic wrap, leaving one corner uncovered. Cook on 100% power. Every 2 minutes flip the chicken around. For 4 to 6 pieces of chicken breasts, cooking time is 4 to 6 minutes or until pink center is gone.

Chocolate:

To melt chocolate, place chocolate pieces in a bowl. Heat uncovered, on 100% power. For 1 cup, heat for 1 to 2 minutes or until soft. Stir every 30 seconds.

Coconut:

To toast the coconut, put desired amount in a bowl. Cook uncovered at 100% power. For 1 cup, cooking time is 2 to 3 minutes or till toasted. Stir every 30 seconds.

Cream Cheese:

To soften, place the cream cheese in a bowl. Heat uncovered at 100%. For 3 ounces heat for 30 seconds or till soft.

Ice Cream:

Softening a frozen pint of ice cream is done by placing the box into the microwave. Open the lid and leave uncovered. Heat at 100% power for 30 seconds or until soft.

Tip: If your microwave doesn't have a turntable, you should rotate foods halfway through cooking.

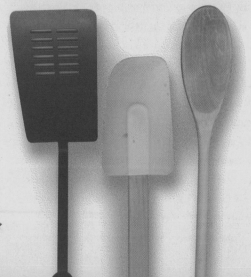

African

recipes for our families from our fathers families

African Cooking

According to the Bible, Africa is the birthplace of mankind. It should not surprise us to learn that it is also the birthplace of all we know in the culinary industry. Each country in Africa created its own unique style of cooking by combining its resources with the wisdom of man and seasoning it with the inspirations given by God. The basic technique for African cooking is similar—very hot spices, well-roasted meats of choice, and an equal balance of fruits and vegetables. It is from this well-combined group of foods and spices that we now have such a vast variety of cooking today.

Traditional African cooking is much more than a style. Cooking is considered sacred and food is prepared with the utmost care and attention to detail. It is prepared with loved ones in mind. Equal care is taken in selecting the ingredients and the preparation. Countries like Liberia, Senegal, Madagascar, Kenya, Sudan, Morocco, Ethiopia, Tanzania, Mozambique, and the Island of Zanzibar all have a wide range of resources that are grown on their own soil. The ingredients these countries produce are found in many recipes around the world. It is clear to see how easily the art of African cooking has been transformed the cultural melting pot. In all of these countries, rice is a staple item served at least once a day—sometimes two or three times—depending on the country.

It is said that the hottest, most peppery food is found in Ethiopia. Liberia is known for such delicious desserts as sweet potato, coconut, and pumpkin pies, and rice bread with mashed bananas. Senegal, Madagascar, and Ethiopia are all known for their tropical and exotic fruits. Morocco is the country known for its plentiful herbs and spices, such as coriander, cumin, saffron, marjoram, sandalwood, and mint.

The art of cooking with spicy herbs and seasonings allows the blood in the body to clean itself of harmful disease. The roasting method of cooking meat is in line with God's instructions to man on how it should be prepared, so that there is no blood remaining in the meat that is eaten. In traditional African cooking, every method had a specific purpose behind it—to satisfy the soul and to prolong life. With this in mind, when our slave ancestors were brought to this country and others, they brought with them their culture and imparted it into their new surroundings, thus creating culinary bridge between cultures.

Flat Bread

Combine both flours and baking powder. Add club soda and water and mix well. In a non-stick pan, heat until pan is medium hot. Place a thin layer of mixture in the pan and cook until one side is light brown. Only cook on one side. Serve warm with soup.

4 cups unbleached self-rising flour

1 cups whole cracked wheat flour

1 teaspoon baking powder

1 cup club soda

4 cups water

Recipes for Living

"Just like I use sour lemons to make sweet lemon pie, through prayer God has shown me that in every sour situation...if brought to Him, He can make the circumstances sweet."

Mrs. Sadie McClep
First Lady, Green Forest Baptist Church
Decatur, GA
Rev. George. O. McClep, Pastor

Whole Wheat Bread

1½ cups warm water (105-115 degrees)

2 packages dry yeast

2 cups whole wheat flour

2 cups unbleached white flour

1 teaspoon salt

2 tablespoons oil

2 tablespoons maple syrup

Place warm water and yeast into a medium bowl, mix with a dough hook until yeast is dissolved into the water. Add flours, salt, oil and maple syrup. Mix on low until all ingredients are combined. Beat on high for 5 min. Turn dough on to floured surface and kneed for 1 minute. Place dough back in bowl and rub a little oil on top to prevent any crusting. Cover with a damp cloth and let rise in a warm place for 2 hours doubling in size. Place dough back on a well-floured surface and cut into 12 equal parts. Roll into balls and place onto a non-stick pan. Let rise for 1 hour. Bake at 350° for 25 minutes.

Yield: 12/2 ounce rolls

Recipes for Living

"Macaroni without cheese is like a Christian without time on his knees! You can do it that way, but it just doesn't have the best results.

Mrs. Jamell Meeks
First Lady, Salem Baptist Church
Chicago, IL

Cooking Up Compassion

Though this recipe is high in calories it is a "heart healthy" recipe that's sure to please. The savor of compassion can be found throughout scripture; however, the book of Lamentations tells us clearly, "It is of the Lord's mercies that we are not consumed, because His compassions fail not; they are new every morning." Are you not glad, my sister, that his compassions do not fail?

Birthed from life's challenges, issues, failures, and victories comes compassion—the kind that becomes the catalyst for change in your surroundings and produces a newness of life that you never knew existed. One main ingredient for the recipe of compassion is the ability to love unconditionally. Typically we place stipulations and limitations on whom we love, how we love and how much love we are willing to share. The aromas of compassion have no boundaries or lack of love. Smell the vapors?

In order to reveal the true flavor, you will have to "cook up" compassion from scratch. From scratch? Yes my friend from scratch! I know that times in which we live have transformed us into a cycle of quickness. Compassion is not phony, it is not masked or quick. It is genuine.

Our great-grandparents knew the very essence of compassion. It took very little for them to realize a need in someone's life. That realization came with a powerful zeal to assist in any way possible. Opening the canals of the heart to just say "I am here for you," means the world to those who often times lack this very important presence in their lives. Compassion is very tangible—not in the sense of the purchase and delivery of a "gift". It is a gift, from the heart of the Lord God to yours. Ezekiel 11:19 says, "I will give them one heart, and I will put a new spirit within you; and I will take the stony heart out of their flesh, and will give them an heart of flesh" (emphasis added). I told you this recipe was "heart healthy." Now for the finishing touches, I will say please my sister, add a pinch of "yielded vessel" and equal parts of "obedience to the voice of God" and you will have the most delectable delicacy mentionable—the true Spirit of Compassion!

(This recipe for life serves endlessly to as many as you desire to serve; once cooked you will never have an empty dish). Sit back relax and enjoy.

Marlow Talton

Minted Iced Tea

1 (Lipton ice tea) tea bag
2 sprigs mint leaves (chopped)
2 quarts boiling water

Add tea bag and chopped mint leaves to boiling water and brew for one hour. Strain off the chopped mint leaves and tea bags. Chill for 3 hours and serve over crushed ice, garnished with a sprig of mint and a thin slice of lemon.

Yield: 2 quarts

Recipes for Living

"As a child growing up in Arkansas and playing outside on a hot summer day, the smell of Momma's candied yams, smothered chicken, collard greens and hot water cornbread would cause me to stop playing and beat a path home to the kitchen. I try to fix good food like that for my congregation, so that we can fellowship together."

Mrs. Marilyn D. Wiley,
First Lady, Rock of Ages Baptist Church,
Maywood, IL
Rev. Wiley, Pastor

Pineapple Punch

Combine all ingredients, stir and chill for 1 hour.
Add crushed ice.

Yield: 1 gallon

2 quarts water
3 cups sugar
1 teaspoon cinnamon
4 whole cloves
4 cups sweet pineapple juice
1 cup orange juice (unsweetened)
1 whole lemon squeezed
4 cups crushed ice

Recipes for Living

"My favorite dish to cook is Macaroni and Cheese.
It's not easy to make, but the care I put into to it
manages to come through in its taste. This dish
always manages to encourage the people I love."

Mrs. Gracie White
Petersburg, VA

Boiling Away the Blues

Having a therapist for a husband has taught me to recognize clinical terms like bipolar disorder or manic depression, (where the individual's mood swings from extreme highs to extreme lows and everything in between). Bipolar disorder is one of those diseases that is often overlooked and not recognized as an illness by the patient, relatives, or friends. People who have it may suffer needlessly for years or even decades. Take a moment to think if this description fits anyone you know. Lift that person's name before God.

Nearly 18 million African Americans experience depression each year, and more than 7 percent will even die from this illness. Depression is not, and should not be, a normal part of life for anyone, but many people believe their symptoms are "just the blues" or evidence of a personal weakness instead of a medical illness.

Why? The most common symptom of depression is change of appetite, often experienced as an increase in appetite and weight gain. Not uncommon when you're under stress most of the time. The depression rate among African American women is estimated to be almost 50% higher than the rate among Caucasian women. Ladies, we have to change this statistic. Yes, its true, cultural background plays a large role in how the symptoms are reported and interpreted, and often plays a critical role in how and if clinical depression is recognized and treated properly.

After reading these hard realities, we have our work cut out for us. We are a special people—one of a kind. The Bible records this symptom in Proverbs 12:25-26, "Heaviness in the heart of man maketh it stoop: but a good word maketh it glad. The righteous is more excellent than his neighbor: but the way of the wicked seduceth them."

When we make erroneous choices in life, we become boiling mad, despondent, blue, skinny of fat, all alone. It is essential that we seek God with our whole heart, obtain his guidance, allow the Holy Spirit to intercede for us. Refuse to allow the enemy of our souls to throw us off balance with God. If we don't love and take care of ourselves, we really can't help anyone else.

If you have affirmed you have this disease, pray and give it to God. Next talk with a professional. Help is available. Celebrate where you are, but seek to get BETTER. Luke 5:31 "And Jesus answering said unto them, They that are whole need not a physician; but they that are sick."

Porcher George

Beans & Raisins

Cook onions and garlic in a hot oil skillet. Add remaining ingredients except beans and rice. Heat to a boil. Reduce heat. Cover and cook for 8 minutes. Stir in beans. – Cook for five more minutes. Serve over rice.

Yield: 4 Servings

2 onions, chopped

1 garlic clove, chopped

½ teaspoon ginger, ground

1 teaspoon cinnamon, ground

1 teaspoon turmeric, ground

½ cup raisins

1 cup chicken broth

1 cup squash, diced

2 cups rice, cooked, hot

1 can (15 ounce) garbanzo beans

Recipes for Living

"Meditation is like simmering a good piece of roast—the longer it cooks, the richer the flavor. If you want the depth of His treasures, you have to stay there awhile."

Karen Waddles
First Lady, Zion Hill Missionary Baptist Church
Chicago, IL
Rev. George Waddles Pastor

Chin-Chin

3 cups flour

1 cup butter or margarine

3 eggs

1½ teaspoons baking powder

1 cup of water

1 cup of milk (or additional cup of water)

6 tablespoons of sugar

Oil

Mix all the ingredients except the oil together. Mix the dough until it is smooth. Place some flour on a cutting board or other flat surface. Place some dough on the cutting board and flatten it until it is about 1/2 inch thick. Cut the dough into little squares, each square about 1/2 inch by 1/2 inch (they are supposed to be like a small piece of candy). Place some oil on the stove on medium heat, and allow the oil to heat up. Once the oil is hot, place a few handfuls of the cut pieces into the oil. (The oil may appear to foam...that is all right, though rotating through it with a utensil will tame it a bit). Allow the chin-chin to deep fry until brown. Some people prefer it light brown, and others dark brown. Place the fried pieces on a napkin to soak up the extra oil.

Yield: 6-8 Servings

Niles Ignatius Ita

Recipes for Living

"When I see a church member is down, I just invite 'em on over for a home cooked meal. Once they get a taste of that soul food of mine, I see a real nice change in them."

Mrs. Lizzie Mae Perry
First Lady, Double Springs Baptist Church
Covington, GA
Rev. Dewey E. Perry, Pastor

Cumin Salad

Heat Rice, Water, Salt to a boil in a skillet. Reduce heat. Cover and simmer 15 for minutes. Remove from heat. Stir. Cover and let sit for 5 minutes. Stir in Butter and Sugar. Dash with Cinnamon.

Yield: 6 Servings

1½ cups Rice
2½ cups Water
½ tsp Salt
⅓ cup Butter
½ cup Sugar, powdered
dash Cinnamon

Recipes for Living

"I pray that the Lord blesses our members meals because when He anoints the food it will be nourishing to the body, soul and mind."

Mrs. Felice Kee
First Lady, New life Fellowship Center
Charlotte, NC
John P. Kee, Pastor

Fried Plantain

4 plantains
(Un-ripe plantains are usually green in color and hard. As they ripen, they become more yellowish in color and a little softer, and when they are getting too ripe, they start to have more and more black patches, and they are really soft).

Vegetable oil

Put oil into a frypan/saucepan, about ? inch high, and place on low heat. Slice or dice each plantain as follows (lay the plantain down, so vertically means cutting along the circumference, and longitudinally means cutting along the length). For larger slices, slice the plantains either vertically, or diagonally, so that each slice is about ? inch thick. For smaller pieces, cut the plantain into two of four parts longitudinally, and then slice vertically. Place the cut pieces into the hot oil, spreading over the bottom of the pan. Turn over when the bottom sides are golden brown in color. (Some people prefer them more yellowish in color, and some more darker brown...any is fine because as long as the heat is low, the plantain will be cooked). Let the other side get as brown as the first side. Remove using a spatula or large spoon. Depending on the ripeness of the plantain, you may want to put the fried plantains on some napkins first to soak up some of the excess oil. This is normally eaten with eggs and toast for breakfast, with coconut rice, or jollof rice.

Yield: 6-8 servings

Niles Ignatius Ita

Basting In Christian Entertainment

"Your eye is the lamp of your body. If your eye is healthy, your whole body is full of light . . ." Luke 11:34

Sisters, have you noticed that what you see, read or hear can have lasting effects on your behavior? The "right" song can put you in the mood to release certain inhibitions. What you see in a movie can be forever embedded in your brain. What you read can conjure up ideas and visions that remain with you. You may even want to duplicate some of the scenarios you've read about in the latest risqué novel. However, as a Christian you must be ever mindful of what you expose your eyes to.

In this day and age of violence and sex in the movies, explicit websites and offensive language in songs, you must be cautious of what you choose to be entertained by. Even though the temptation may be great to "indulge just a little", you set examples for others without knowing it. Could you recommend the latest book you've read to another sister in Christ without being embarrassed? Could you loan one of your favorite songs to your pastor? If Jesus appeared in the movie theatre where you sat, what would you want to be watching?

In the ever-widening sea of entertainment choices available, you must navigate with purpose to find options that will have positive effects on your mind, body and soul. Now, more than ever there are books, websites, and music that do not tend to offend, but uplift,

encourage, and support you as a resilient black female. As busy women, you are taking care of work, family, and home, and have precious little time for yourself. Spend this time wisely on recreation that allows you to grow deep in your spirituality, and allows you to share your experiences with other sisters. Resources like Sister to Sister: Devotions for and from African American Women, www.blackandchristian.com, and www.niaonline.com are available just to name a few. Create lasting and positive memories for yourself by choosing to baste in entertainment with your best interest in mind. After all, you deserve it. You are a high priestess worthy of the best. Choose accordingly.

Linda Peavy

Ginger Root Greens

1 carton (12 ounces) cottage cheese

4 tablespoons butter

1 clove garlic, cut into two pieces

½ teaspoon pepper

¼ teaspoon ginger, ground

⅛ teaspoon cinnamon, ground

⅛ teaspoon cloves, ground

2 tablespoons onion, minced

1 green chili, chopped

2 teaspoons gingerroot

2 pounds collard greens, fresh and chopped

Put cottage cheese, 2 tablespoons butter, garlic, pepper, ginger, cinnamon, and cloves in a bowl and stir. Preheat oven for 300 degrees. Let stand for 20 minutes. Take garlic out. Cook onion, chili, gingerroot, and collard greens in 2 tablespoons butter in oven until tender – approx 30 minutes. Drain. Serve collards over cottage cheese mixture.

Yield: 6 Servings

Recipes for Living

"God is the Ultimate Baker and once he puts everthing together; the end result is always "A slice of Heaven"! Romans 8:28 "And we know that all things work together for good to them that love God, to them that are the called according to His purpose".

Mrs. Vickie V. Person
First Lady: Cathedral of Holy Bible Church
Chicago, Illinois
Rev. Dr. Booker J. Person, Pastor

Jollof Rice

Rinse the rice. Put the rice and about 6 cups of water into a pot and place on high heat. If you are using fresh ingredients (the tomatoes and pepper) blend them until they are smooth in texture (you can also grind the onion with this mixture). Let the rice cook 10-15 minutes. Add either the tomato/pepper mixture or the tomato sauce and tomato paste and the onion, if it hasn't been added yet. Add enough water or meat broth to allow the rice to complete cooking – approx. 10 minutes (since you will not be draining the rice, it is better to add too little and check up on it often, than to add too much). If you use water, add 4 magi cubes for taste. Add salt and cayenne pepper (as the rice is cooking, or as you are eating the finished product, you can add more of either one of these). Allow the rice to continue cooking until the rice is soft—approx. 10 minutes. If it is not dry at this point, then switch the heat to low to allow it to dry the excess water without making the rice much softer. Once cooked, add more salt or pepper to it if you wish. Normally eaten with some sort of meat on the side

Coconut Rice
Repeat everything as stated previously, but replace the meat broth with Chaokoh coconut milk (unless you can make fresh coconut milk with the blender). Do not use the second option of tomato paste. This ingredient is not required nor necessary for coconut rice.

4 cups white rice

6 cups water

2 tomatoes and 1 bell pepper (without seeds if you don't like things too hot) or 8 ounces canned tomato sauce and 3 ounces canned tomato paste

1 onion, sliced or diced

2 teaspoon salt

1 teaspoon cayenne pepper

1 cup meat broth or water

Yield: 6-8 Servings   Niles Ignatius Ita

African Peanut Chicken

2 pounds chicken breast, boneless, skinless

1 onion, chopped

1½ pounds sweet potatoes, cubed

3 cups hot water

1 cup peanut butter

2 tablespoons cooking oil

1 red pepper, chopped

3 garlic cloves, chopped

1 can (14 ounces) tomatoes, diced

1½ teaspoons cayenne pepper

2 teaspoons salt

1 pound spinach, drained

Rice, cooked

Season chicken breasts with dash of salt and pepper and sauté with onion. When chicken browns, remove from skillet. Leave oil in skillet. In a small pot cook sweet potatoes until tender. Wisk together hot water and peanut butter. Add remaining ingredients except rice to skillet and sauté. Add chicken and stir. Then add peanut butter mixture and let simmer at low heat for 15 minutes. Add sweet potatoes to chicken mixture. Continue to simmer for 15 minutes then serve hot over rice.

Yield: 6 Servings
The Ultimate Event

Recipes for Living

"Prayer and meditation on God's word are like beans and cornbread—they're good to you and good for you."

Karen Waddles
First Lady, Zion Hill Missionary Baptist Church
Chicago, IL
Rev. George Waddles Pastor

African Peanut Rice
recipe on page 24

25

Conch Salad

(pronounced "conk")

2 pounds cooked
   conch meat

1 tomato

1 bell pepper

1 small onion

3 lemons

3 limes

1 tablespoon of salt

½ teaspoon of crushed
   red pepper

Dice conch meat, tomato, bell pepper and onion. Pour ingredients into a medium size bowl. Squeeze juice from lemons and limes over ingredients. Sprinkle salt and crushed red pepper. Mix well.

Yield: 4 Servings

Lonnie Perriman

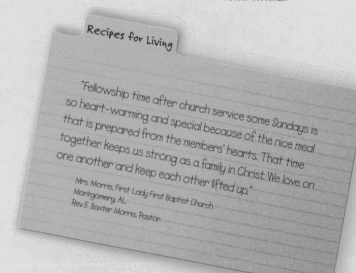

Recipes for Living

"Fellowship time after church service some Sundays is so heart-warming and special because of the nice meal that is prepared from the members' hearts. That time together keeps us strong as a family in Christ. We love on one another and keep each other lifted up."

Mrs. Morris, First Lady First Baptist Church
Montgomery, AL
Rev. E. Baxter Morris, Pastor

Crushing Out Colds

So ladies, I hear you're battling a cold. Trying to balance a cold and a hectic schedule is not very easy. If you are like me, you don't even take the time to nature your self or your cold, you just turn your body on automatic and it just runs and runs. A woman's basic instinct is to make sure everything is taken care of and running smoothly. So you work all day; go home and care for your household, and finally, when you have a moment to your self (usually late at night) you just drift off to sleep. These strenuous daily routines often cause our body to weaken in its attempt to fight off those nasty colds that drag us down even further. You need to STOP and take some time for yourself. Learn to nurture yourself and supply your body with the right nutrients to fight off the germs.

Medical doctors have taken an oath in their profession, an oath that prevents them from marketing the natural herbs and vitamins that our bodies desperately need. That is why we need to become more educated about existing health products that can heal and energize our bodies naturally. Here are a few tips that help me when I find myself coming down with a cold. As women, we know our bodies and we can tell when something just isn't right. We might wake up a little more drowsy than normal, or we may have clear symptoms— a runny nose or a scratchy throat. You should immediately get some Echinacea-Golden Seal, a natural medicine, in your system. Echinacea builds the immune system and Golden Seal is a natural antibiotic. A lot of people don't know about this natural medicine but it has helped me a great deal. It doesn't matter if it's just a runny nose or a hacking cough, you can naturally get your body back in order. Another great natural medicine to take if you feel like you're coming down with the flu is Oscillococcinum, which also works on your immune system to help you fight off symptoms such as fever, chill, body aches and pains. Oscillococcinum can be taken even when you're not sure it's the Flu but you know its something. Remember Ladies to also replenish your body with vitamin C, 500-1000mg per day while fighting a cold and drink plenty of liquids preferably clear or light in color without a lot of sugar. How ever if you run a fever for more than 24 hours, you need to consult a physician.

We all love to have fun, feel good and enjoy our families. In order to do these things, you need to, first, take care of yourself. Check with a nutrition store for a multi-vitamin that you can take daily, one that will supply your body with all the nutrients it needs. Don't take your health for granted and remember; you are the most important person in your life. Take care of yourself and enjoy life to its fullest.

Jeanette Taylor

Ethiopian Pepper Beef

2 red peppers, diced

2 jalepeno pepper, chopped

⅓ cup dry wine

3 garlic cloves, cut into fourths

½ teaspoon cardamom, ground

1½ teaspoons salt

1 tablespoon gingerroot, chopped

1 teaspoon turmeric, ground

1 tablespoon butter

1 tablespoon cooking oil

2 pounds beef sirloin, boneless strips

2 onions, chopped

1 red pepper, sliced

2 cups rice, cooked

Blend peppers, jalepeno peppers, wine, garlic, cardamom, salt, gingerroot, and turmeric. Heat butter and oil in a skillet on the stove. Stir in beef and cook for 15 minutes. Remove beef. Cook and stir onion and pepper strips in remaining oil. Add blender mixture and stir. Add the beef and stir. Heat to a boil. Reduce heat. Simmer uncovered for 15 minutes. Serve with rice.

Yield: 6 Servings

Recipes for Living

"Hospitality, good food prepared with lots of love, is what you expect when you visit my house."

Karen Greenup
First Lady of Christ The Deliverer Assembly
Denham Springs, Louisiana
Rev. Greenup

Ghana Beef Soup

Place beef, water, red pepper, salt, and ginger in a crock pot. Bring to a boil. Reduce heat. Cover and simmer for 1 hour. Add squash and cook for one more hour. Add tomatoes and beans and cook for 20 minutes. Serve over rice.

Yield: 6 Servings

1½ pounds beef, chuck, boneless (cut into cubes)

2 cups water

¼ teaspoon red pepper, ground

2 teaspoon salt

¼ teaspoon ginger, ground

1½ pounds squash, blended

2 tomatoes, chopped

1 package (10 ounces) lima beans, frozen

Recipes for Living

"Being a pastor's wife doesn't mean you lose your own identity, it means you rely more on your own identity."

Linda Lewis
First Lady,
Agape Temple Church

Kenya Halibut

1 onion, sliced

2 garlic cloves, chopped

2 jalapeno peppers, chopped

½ teaspoon salt

¾ teaspoon coriander, ground

2 tablespoons vinegar

2 tablespoons cooking oil

4 halibut steaks

Preheat oven for 350 degrees. In a hot oil skillet cook onions, garlic, and peppers. Reduce heat and mix in everything else but fish. Simmer for 5 minutes. Put fish in a baking dish. Coat fish with mixture. Cook uncovered for 30 minutes.

Yield: 4 Servings

Recipes for Living

"After years of being a dedicated mother, pastor's wife, and minister, I have decided that what is most important is that my children, my husband, and others to whom I minister, should see Christ in me."

Malinda Scott,
First Lady, Pillar of Truth Church

Lemon Moroccan Chicken

Preheat oven to 350 degrees.

Mix cilantro, paprika, garlic, ginger, turmeric, salt, and cumin. Rub mixture on chicken. Sprinkle with flour. Put chicken in an ungreased dish. Mix water, lemon juice, and bouillon. Pour liquid mix over chicken. Add olives and lemon slices.

Cook uncovered for 1 hour.

Yield: 6 Servings

¼ cup cilantro

1 tablespoon paprika

2 garlic cloves, minced

½ teaspoon ginger

½ teaspoon turmeric, ground

½ teaspoon salt

2 teaspoons cumin, ground

3 pounds chicken, broiler-fryer, (cut up)

⅓ cup flour

½ cup water

¼ cup lemon juice

1 teaspoon chicken bouillon

½ cup Greek olives

1 lemon, sliced

31

Samboska

- 1½ pounds ground beef
- 1 onions, chopped
- 1 garlic, minced
- ½ cup almonds, slivered
- 1 teaspoon sugar
- 1 teaspoon salt
- 1 teaspoon curry powder
- 1 tablespoon vinegar
- 1 teaspoon lemon juice
- 1 tablespoon cooking oil
- 1 package puff pastry dough

Preheat oven 350 degrees. In large frying pan brown ground beef. Pour off half the liquid from beef. Add remaining ingredients except puff pastry. Saute until no pink remains in the beef. Set to the side. Cut puff pastry into 3 inch by 3 inch squares. Brush with oil. Add meat mixture to the middle of the pastry shell. Fold and form a triangle. Bake in oven until brown – approx. 10 minutes

Yield: 6 Servings
The Ultimate Event

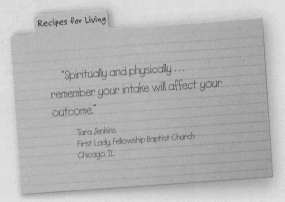

Recipes for Living

"Spiritually and physically . . . remember your intake will affect your outcome."

Tara Jenkins
First Lady, Fellowship Baptist Church
Chicago, IL

Steaming Up Romance

How do you keep the music playing in you marriage? How do you make the love you felt when you said, 'I do' last? How do you keep the passion from fading too fast? Good questions, with many different answers. The key ingredient to steaming up romance is to just do something daily to let your husband know how much he means to you.

In Hebrews 13:4 it says , "the marriage bed is undefiled." Undefiled means anything goes. If your husband wants the two of you to try something new and it isn't degrading...try it. One suggestion I have is that you talk to your mate. Ask him the tough questions. Get an evaluation of how he thinks you're doing in that area. If you are bored in the romance area of your marriage, communicate that to him as well. You both need to be on one accord to keep each other happy.

I remember three years ago when I was writing my first adult novel, FLAME. Though it was a Christian fiction piece, I was determined to make it juicy. I wanted a real page turner. One of my friends was on my reading pool and I must have hit my objective because I remember her saying, "Oh my gosh girl, reading this made me want to have better intimacy with my husband." Of course I smiled, feeling all proud. But then she said, "Your marriage bed must be the bomb." I felt such conviction. I had given so much thought into my characters love lives, that I had neglected my own. From that moment on, I prayed and asked God to make my love life more juicer than anything I could ever write.

So I felt led to talk to my husband. I communicated to him that I wanted his attention after the actual act was over and I needed more romance all the time. He vented that her wanted a cleaner house and eatable meals. After we both pleased each other in area outside of the bedroom, we started dating all over again. Then I heard the music play. I was so in love with my man again. The passion in the bedroom was on!

So ladies if you need to steam things up a bit in the love department, I say pray, talk, fix it, date, and then...turn the heat all the way up!

Stephanie Perry Moore

Seafood Paella

1½ pounds shrimp, shelled, deveined

12 clams, washed

6 mussels, washed

1 onion, chopped

1 green pepper, chopped

1 tomato, diced

1 can green peas

1 cup rice

2 cups water

1 teaspoon seasoning salt

½ teaspoon saffron, crushed

1 teaspoon parsley

½ teaspoon pepper

1 pinch garlic

½ teaspoon thyme, whole

Preheat oven 350 degrees. In a large casserole dish, stir in all ingredients. Cover with aluminum foil. Place in oven and cook until rice is tender and clams and mussels open up – approx 10 minutes.

Yield: 8 Servings
The Ultimate Event

Recipes for Living

"Feasting on bread will bring extra pounds to your physical body. Feasting on the bread of heaven will bring extra pounds to your spiritual body."

Lisa T. Ballard
First Lady, Sunrise Baptist Church
Chicago, IL

Seafood Paella
recipe on page 34

Tagine Lamb

3 pounds lamb, boneless and cubed

2 tablespoons cooking oil

1 onion, chopped

¼ teaspoon saffron

½ teaspoon cinnamon, ground

½ teaspoon pepper

1 teaspoon salt

2 garlic cloves, minced

2 cups water

1 tablespoon honey

In a large skillet, cook lamb and oil. Cook for 20 minutes.

Mix in onion, saffron, cinnamon, pepper, salt, and garlic.

Stir in water and honey. Heat to a boil.

Reduce heat. Cover and simmer for 30 minutes.

Yield: 8 Servings

Recipes for Living

"A good spiritual meal is comforting to the soul and satisfying to the Spirit."

Monica Arnold
First Lady, New Horizon Worship Center
Jersey City, NJ
Pastor Michael Arnold

West African Shrimp

Pepper Paste:
Blend all ingredients except paprika.
Put paprika in a pan on the stove and heat.
Pour blender mixture into the pot. Let cool.

Mix chili sauce and red pepper paste.
Serve with chilled shrimp.

Yield: 6 Servings

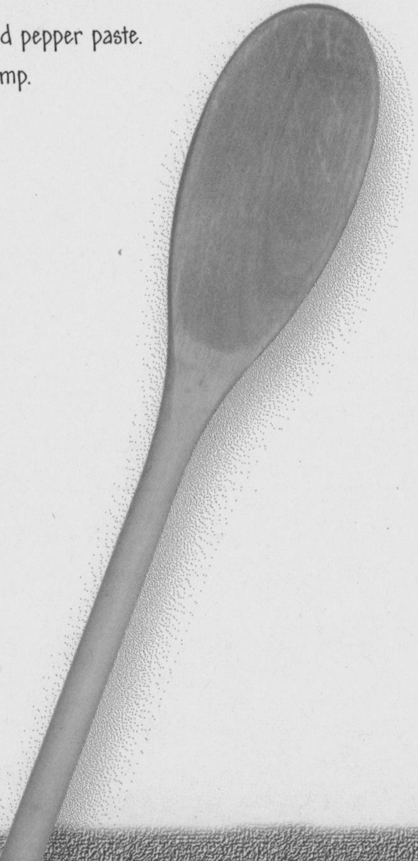

12 large shrimp, chilled, cooked
1 cup chili sauce
2 tablespoons pepper paste

Pepper Paste
1 teaspoon red pepper
⅛ onion, minced
¾ teaspoon salt
¼ teaspoon ginger, ground
¼ cup red wine
⅛ teaspoon cardamom, ground
⅛ cloves, ground
⅛ teaspoon coriander, ground
⅛ teaspoon nutmeg, ground
⅛ teaspoon cinnamon, ground
⅛ tsp black pepper
1 garlic clove
¼ cup paprika

Almond-Date Torte

1 package (8 ounce)
pitted dates, chopped

1⅓ cups evaporated milk

1⅓ cups sugar

4 beaten egg yokes

½ cup butter

1 teaspoon vanilla

2 teaspoons cornstarch

3 tablespoons cold water

1 cup toasted almonds

2 packages (24 count)
lady fingers

Cook and stir dates, milk, sugar, yokes, butter, and vanilla over heat until thick. Dissolve cornstarch in water. Add to egg/milk mixture and stir until mixture thickens even more. Add almonds. Line the bottom and sides of a 9-inch spring form pan with the lady fingers, and pour filling into pan up to the rim of the pan. Chill for 4 hours. Remove sides from pan, top with Cool Whip, and serve cold. Garnish with fresh strawberries.

Yield: 1 9-inch cake

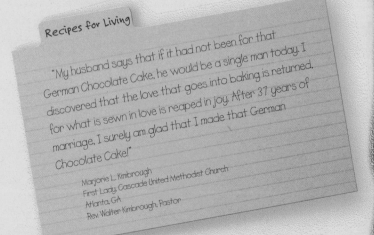

Recipes for Living

"My husband says that if it had not been for that German Chocolate Cake, he would be a single man today. I discovered that the love that goes into baking is returned, for what is sewn in love is reaped in joy. After 37 years of marriage, I surely am glad that I made that German Chocolate Cake!"

Marjorie L. Kimbrough
First Lady, Cascade United Methodist Church
Atlanta, GA
Rev. Walter Kimbrough, Pastor

Eating More Ethics

Early that Sunday morning our women's Sunday school class had engaged in a challenging discussion of the importance of living out our faith in a world that has little tolerance for the gospel. The worship service was moving. The choir sang Zion's songs with unusual fervor, moving the members to a state of high praise. And the message was so powerful that we were almost thrust into the very portals of heaven. Everyone left worship that day talking about how we "really had church."

Later that afternoon my daughter and I decided to run to a shopping mall. As we pulled into the parking lot I spied out my parking space! It was only four spaces from the front door. What a gift from God! But straight ahead, I saw another car approaching from the other direction and seemingly headed for my parking space. The race was on. I gunned the engine and raced at unnerving speed and careened into the parking space just ahead of the other car. With a shout of glee I said, "I know she didn't think she was going to get that parking space!" I glanced to my right and noticed a strange look on my daughter's face. I was puzzled. I was expecting at least a high-five. She looked at me and said simply, "Mom, weren't you teaching us this morning in Sunday school about the importance of giving up our rights and putting others first? Didn't you say that has something to do with our witness?"

I was ashamed and she was right. The truth of the matter is that the power of the Christian life is not in the fervor of our worship experiences; it is not in simply knowing right from wrong; it is not having a storehouse of memorized scripture to quote in the time of need; nor is it the ability to speak powerfully or sing like the angelic choir. The true power of the Christian life is in making decisions and living lives moment by moment— in parking lots, in church business meetings, at the beauty salon, and even at home—that literally shine forth his presence and dismiss the pervasive darkness of this world. At the end of the day, what difference has Christ made in my life that has been seen or felt by others? It's not how loud the shout – but rather how worthy the walk!

Karen Waddles

Baked Bananas

4 large bananas, skin on

4 tablespoons brown sugar

2 tablespoons butter

1 teaspoon pineapple juice

Bake bananas at 350 degrees until the skin is black – approx. 10 min. in color. Peel and set aside. In a saucepan melt brown sugar, butter, and pineapple juice. Slice baked bananas and add to hot mixture. Serve warm and top with whip topping.

Yield: 4 servings

Recipes for Living

"The food you eat must be digested to benefit your body. So must the spiritual food you eat also. You shouldn't just receive a good Word (preaching, teaching, or ministry), but you must digest it by walking in the manifestation of the Word."

Beverly L. Wilson
First Lady, Valley Kingdom Ministries International
South Holland, IL

Banana Cream Parfait

In a medium saucepan, place egg yolks, rum, sugar, heavy cream, and nutmeg. Bring to a boil, stirring constantly until thick. Let cool. Whip egg whites to a peek and fold into cool custard mixture. Spoon into a parfait glass alternating custard and bananas; garnish with a ladyfinger. Serve cold.

Yield: 5 servings

3 eggs, separated
2 tablespoons rum
2 tablespoons sugar
1 cup heavy cream
    Nutmeg (to taste)
5 bananas, sliced
5 lady fingers

Mango-Lime Cake

Cake:

1¼ cups granulated sugar

1¾ cups cake flour

½ teaspoon baking powder

½ teaspoon salt

1½ sticks butter, softened

½ cup buttermilk

3 eggs

1 tablespoon lime juice

1 tablespoon lime zest

Filling:

1¼ cups mango puree

1 cup chopped mango

4½ ounces white chocolate

¼ cup lime juice

3 teaspoons powder gelatin

1 cup heavy cream

1½ cups granulated sugar

Cake: Sift dry ingredients. Add butter and buttermilk slowly; then beat for 1 minute on second speed. And eggs, lime juice, and zest slowly; then mix on low for 1 minute. Pour into a greased 10-inch cake pan and bake at 350° for 35 minutes or until done. Dump and let cool completely.

Filling: Warm mango puree and chopped mango and set aside. Melt white chocolate and set aside. Place lime juice and gelatin in a small bowl and heat in microwave for 2 minutes until gelatin is completely dissolved. Add gelatin mixture to warm mango puree. Add gelatin and puree mixture to warm white chocolate and set aside. Whip heavy cream and sugar to a soft peak using an electric mixer. Fold whipped cream into puree mixture. Slice cake into two. Using a spring form pan, place half the cake on the bottom of pan, fill to the rim with mango-lime mixture and place the other half cake slice on top. Chill remaining filling for later use. Chill cake for 2 hours. After chilled, remove from pan and spread remaining filling over entire cake. Garnish with fresh limes and mango slices.

Yield: 1 10-inch cake

Tapioca Pudding

2 cups milk
¼ cup tapioca
¼ cup butter
¼ teaspoon salt
1 ounce egg yolk
½ cup granulated sugar
¼ lemon rind
(grated fine)
½ teaspoon vanilla
1 ounce egg whites

Soak tapioca for 1 hour in half of the milk. Bring the remaining milk to a boil and add the soaked tapioca, butter, and salt. Boil until tapioca is done – approx. 5 min.. Cream egg yokes and half the sugar, and all of the lemon rind and vanilla. Then add to boiling tapioca. Beat egg whites and remaining sugar to a medium froth and fold into boiling mixture while still on the heat. Pour into 4 buttered and sugared 3-ounce baking dishes, and brown in oven at 450 degrees. Serve warm.

Yield: 4 Servings

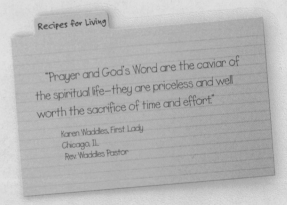

Recipes for Living

"Prayer and God's Word are the caviar of the spiritual life—they are priceless and well worth the sacrifice of time and effort."

Karen Waddles, First Lady
Chicago, IL
Rev. Waddles Pastor

Creole ♡

recipes that mix the spice of life with the soul of the south

Creole Cooking

When it comes to the spicing up of dishes, creole cooking is the one style of cuisine that is most like that of African food. As time elapsed, the migration from Africa into other regions of the world spread like wild fire. Imparting the rich culture and ideas into new worlds was very exciting.

"Creole" cookin in New Orleans is a result of the intermarriages of the cultures that settled in the city, mainly the French, Africans, and Spanish. This style of cooking is a combination of African with a European twist. The dishes are spicy and include bisques and rice dishes filled with the chickens and sausages brought by the settlers and enriched by the delta treasures—crabs, crawfish, oysters, shrimp, and fish. Creole merges a variety of cultures into a rich, unique cuisine with a language all its own—jambalaya, gumbo, "dirty" rice, "blackened" chicken, and fish. The idea behind creole cooking is to feast, be merry, and enjoy your brother's company. A key ingredient in creole cooking is okra, a plant from the soils of Africa.

Today, African Americans maintain a significant role in the continued development of creole cooking. Creole is a combination of diverse people with unique cultures. These people were not afraid to share their ideas, styles and talents. Creole cooking is just another method people created to duplicate their traditional dishes with New World products.

Most creole desserts contain bourbon or rum. The cooking actually evaporates the alcohol, unless the dessert is soaked in or drizzled with it after baking. Many desserts are prepared with pecans and brown sugar, creating that praline flavor. Fresh berries are often used to garnish these desserts in an effort to add color and lighten them up, since many of the desserts are light to medium brown in color. Sauces are used to

Creole Cornbread

Heat oven to 400 degrees. Grease an 8- or 9-inch pan. Combine dry ingredients. Stir in egg yolks, milk, butter and creamed corn until dry ingredients are moist, but not over mixed. Pour batter into prepared pan and bake in the center of the oven for 20-25 minutes until cornbread is light golden brown. Test by inserting a wooden pick into the center.

Yield: 12 Servings

1¼ cups of corn meal

1¼ cups flour

1 teaspoon of baking powder

½ teaspoon salt (optional)

1 tablespoon jalapeno peppers, chopped fine

¼ cup of sugar

4 egg yokes

1 cup milk

2 sticks of butter, softened

1 can creamed corn

Recipes for Living

"The effort my wife puts into her cooking is an indication of her love for me."

Mel Banks
Founder & Chairman of the Board, Urban Ministries
Chicago, IL
Married many years

Honey Wheat Beer Bread

2 bottles of beer (any brand)

1¾ pound cake yeast

1 cup honey

½ cup oil

6 cups bread flour

4 cups whole wheat flour

1 cup cracked wheat

½ tablespoon salt

Combine all ingredients in a 5-quart or more mixing bowl and let rest for 10 minutes. Mix on 1st speed for 1 minute, then using the dough hook on medium speed for 10 minutes. Place on well-floured surface, kneed for 2 minutes forming a ball, and place dough back into bowl, brushing a little oil over the top to prevent a crust from forming. Cover bowl with a damp cloth and allow dough to double in size in a warm place for 2 to 3 hours. Place dough back onto a well-floured surface and cut into four pieces. Grease 4 4-ounce loaf pans. Shape into logs the length of the pan, brush with egg wash, place in pans, and let rise for 2 hours doubling in size. Bake at 325 degrees for 1 hour until golden brown.

Serve warm with honey butter.

Yield: 4-4 oz loaf pans

Ginger Fruit Tea

Pour all ingredients into a big pot. Place cinnamon, nutmeg, and ginger into the pot. Heat for 20 minutes on the stove. Serve hot.

Yield: 8 Servings

2 quarts cranberry juice

1 (6 ounce) can lemonade, frozen, thawed, undiluted

1 (4.5 ounce) can pineapple juice —2 cups apple juice

1 cup orange juice

4 (3 inch) cinnamon sticks

3 nutmegs, whole

1½ teaspoon ginger, ground

Recipes for Living

"What can I say...I'm married to the best Home Economics teacher in the world. I eat real good!"

Dr. Franklin Perry Sr.
Sumter County Schools Superintendent
Americus, GA
Married 33 years

Zesty Party Punch

2 (6 ounce) cans pink lemonade

2 pints vanilla ice cream

1 quart milk

Red food coloring

Turn lemonade into punch bowl. Add 1 pint ice cream. Beat until smooth. Tint milk with food coloring. Stir into lemonade mixture. Scoop remaining ice cream into punch.

Yield: Serves 12

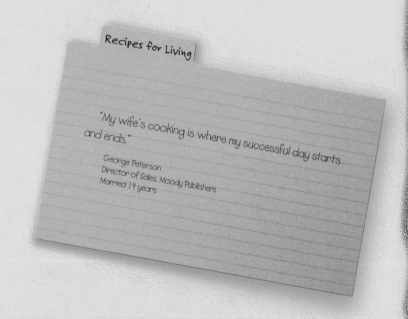

Recipes for Living

"My wife's cooking is where my successful day starts and ends."

George Peterson
Director of Sales, Moody Publishers
Married 14 years

Cranberry Salad

Dissolve Jello in boiling water and rum. Let stand until almost think – approx. 15 minutes. Add cranberry sauce and sour cream.
Fold in celery and nuts.
Then refrigerate until ready to serve.

Yield: 6 Servings

7 packages Jello (Cherry, Strawberry or black cherry)
2 cups boiling water
¼ tablespoon rum
1 can cranberry sauce
1 (8 ounce) carton sour cream
½ cup nuts
½ cup celery, chopped

Recipes for Living

"Though my wife isn't a gourmet, the love she puts into her efforts warms my heart and fills my stomach."

Derrick Moore
Chaplain, Ga. Tech Football Team & Author
Conyers, GA
Married 8 years

Freezing Precious Memories

We all have a past. For some of us our past brings us fond memories, while for others our past is one of pain and regret. Regardless of what our past memories may bring, we have to let go. We can't relive the good ole' days and we can't change the bad ones.

For those whose past is anything but happy memories, it is especially critical to learn to let go. You can't hold on to things that are behind you, but you can hold on to things that are with you. If the pain of yesterday is still effecting your today, then your pain is not your past but your partner. You cannot comfortably walk forward while looking backwards. If you are still being hindered today by circumstances and situations that occurred years ago then you have not let go—and letting go can often be the hardest part. Why? Because we learn to adapt to our painful environment; once we adapt we become comfortable, once we become comfortable we become accepting, once we become accepting we become defined by all the things that created the environment.

Letting go of the past is like ending a relationship. It's hard to part ways with someone you love. You may say, "but I don't love my painful past." If that were so, it should be easy then to simply let it go. Those whom we have become close to, those that we have spent many years with and those who we formed relationships with, are the same ones we have a hard time walking away from. Of course even though all of those relationships are not healthy ones, parting ways may still be hard to do. It's not hard to leave someone or something you have no relationship with.

Holding on to your past decreases your hope in life. Your past emotional hurt, rejection, abuse, abandonment and/or frustration can easily bring you to the point of not expecting much out of life or people. If you don't expect much then you're not disappointed when you don't get much. Letting go is difficult because it ushers you into a new world of hopeful expectations. It changes your partnership.

So you ask, "How do I begin to let go?" Let me say start by saying "exposure!" If you have a piece of meat and put it in a zip lock bag and place it in the freezer for a period of time, it will become frozen. Because it was protected, the meat can be taken out of the freezer, unthawed, and used for its intended purpose – to provide food to the body. However, if you put the same meat in the freezer unprotected and exposed, it will still freeze, but it will eventually become freezer burned. Even when it becomes thawed out, it cannot be used for its intended purpose. That's exactly what you have to do with your past hurts – expose them. Stop covering them up, protecting them, and acting as if they are not there. Stop nurturing them. Ask God to bring someone into your life that you can begin to share your struggles with. Once your pains are exposed, they will become "freezer burned;" when someone or something attempts to thaw out your past, you will realize that your past cannot be used for its intended purpose to hinder you and stop you from living the way God intended for you to live. You will begin to expect to receive all the hope and blessings that God has for you. You will no longer partner with pain but you will partner with praise because you are pressing forward.

Throw out those old freezer-burned memories and go shopping for the fresh life God has for you. IT'S TIME TO LIVE!

Jessica H. Love

Creole Scrambled Eggs

3 tablespoons cooking oil
2 green peppers, sliced
1 onion, sliced
½ teaspoon thyme
1 garlic clove, chopped
2 teaspoons salt
2 tomatoes, chopped
8 eggs
½ milk
½ cup ham, chopped
¼ teaspoon pepper

In a skillet, add 1 tablespoon oil and cook peppers, onions, thyme, garlic and 1/2 teaspoon salt. Heat for 5 minutes. Add tomatoes and cook for 2 minutes. Drain. Place on a plate. Mix all other ingredients with remaining oil. Cook uncovered over low heat. Stir frequently. Mix eggs with vegetables and serve.

Yield: 4 Servings

Recipes for Living

"The detail of my wife's handiwork in the preparation of a simple slaw dog is a reminder that the most minuscule aspects of a relationship merit the greatest attention..."

Jonathan Bellamy
Staffing Recruiter
Atlanta, GA
Married 5 years

Orleans Lettuce Soup

Cook onions in skillet with butter. Reserve 1 cup lettuce. Pour remaining lettuce into skillet. Cover and cook for 5 minutes. Stir in flour and cook for 1 minute. Add water and bouillon and cook for 1 minute. Pour mixture into a blender. Blend for 30 second. Pour back into skillet with remaining lettuce, half and half, salt, and pepper. Heat to a boil and then serve.
Garnish with mint leaves.

Yield: 6 Servings

6 cups (2 small heads) Boston lettuce, shredded
¼ cup flour
3 cups water
1 tablespoon chicken bouillon
1 cup half and half
1 onion, chopped
¼ cup butter
½ teaspoon salt
⅛ teaspoon pepper
Mint leaves

Recipes for Living

"Ingredients of a good marriage are like ingredients in good cooking. If you don't put in the right stuff everything is all messed up."

Henri Hardison
Product Specialist, R.H. Boyd Publishing Corp.
Nashville, TN
Married 29 years

Bourbon Salad

1 head Boston lettuce, pieces

1 package (10 ounce) French-style green beans, cooked

2 tomatoes, cut

2 eggs, boiled and cut

1 can (6½ oz) tuna, drained

8 ripe olives

1 can (2 ounces) anchovy filets, drained

¼ tablespoon rum

Vinaigrette dressing

Combine all ingredients. Toss and serve.

Yield: 4 Servings

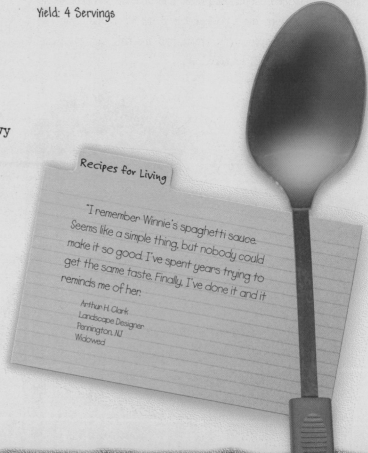

Recipes for Living

"I remember Winnie's spaghetti sauce. Seems like a simple thing, but nobody could make it so good. I've spent years trying to get the same taste. Finally, I've done it and it reminds me of her.

Arthur H. Clark
Landscape Designer
Pennington, NJ
Widowed

Cajun Glazed Ham

Preheat oven to 350 degrees. In a bowl, combine all ingredients, except ham and the pineapple slices. Mix well. Place ham in a roasting pan and baste with mixture.
Bake at 350 degrees for one hour.
To serve, slice ham and place a 1/2 slice of pineapple on each slice.

Yield: 10 Servings

1¼ cup mustard Creole
1 cup brown sugar
¾ cup cane syrup (or corn)
⅓ cup pineapple juice
½ teaspoon cloves, ground
½ teaspoon paprika
½ teaspoon allspice
½ teaspoon nutmeg
½ teaspoon chervil
1 teaspoon garlic, granulated
½ teaspoon cinnamon
5 pounds cured ham
5 pineapple slices, cut in half

Recipes for Living

"Neither one of us cook that often, but when we make a meal together it makes our marriage special."

Rev. Tyrone Carter
President, The Pastor's Network
Markham, IL
Married 7 years

Chili Con Carne

1 onion, chopped

1 garlic clove

2 tablespoons bacon drippings

1 pound beef, ground

1 tablespoon paprika

1 tablespoon chili powder

¼ teaspoon pepper

1 teaspoon salt

1 can tomatoes

1 can kidney beans

3 tablespoons flour

¼ cup water

Saute onions and garlic in bacon drippings until light yellow. Remove from pan and set aside. Add ground beef and cook, stirring until brown. Add seasonings, garlic, and onions. Next, add tomatoes and beans. Cover and simmer for 30 minutes. Blend flour and water together and add to pan.

Simmer an additional 10 minutes.

Portions: 8 Servings

Recipes for Living

"I fell in love with my wife when she fixed me my first dish."

Antonio London
Owner, London's Clothier and Former NFL Player
Houston, TX
Married 8 years

Seasoning Friendships

I grew up wanting a best friend. My older sister was, and is, great. I love her deeply, but when we were growing up, she was more "Mom" than "Girlfriend" and I wanted a good girlfriend. Instinctively, I knew I wanted to tell my business, laugh out loud, share secrets, play dress up, double-date, and sip tea together with my girly kindred. Don't get me wrong, I just wanted to belong. I always cultivated great friendships, but then they would fall out with the rest of the click or get a boyfriend or move away. That kind of unceremonious change always left me wanting. I came to accept such changes as simple facts of life. I figured folks were disposable, fast-food-flings, and just like they kept moving away from me, I could just as easily move away from them. I was wrong and had to learn that "a friend loveth at all times" (Prov. 17:17).

Good friends, real friends, true-blue-I'm-there-for-you friends are precious, the rarest commodity known to woman. Like bread, they will give you sustenance. Like water, they will offer you an oasis in times of trouble and ripple with reflections of yourself. Like an apple, you will need them every day to be healthy. Like wine, they will make you giddy and forget whoever you think you are supposed to be and get you to reveal who you really are. Like chocolate, they will sweeten your life and remind you occasional indulgence is a necessity. Like manna, they will fill your spirit with what you need exactly when you need it, fill your cup when it runneth dry. And in return for such emotional and physical sustenance, what is your offering to this soul food harvest?

You must offer the comfort and warm hearth of your love. You must liberally sprinkle your tears of joy over their triumphs. You must hold tight and bind that which wants to pull away from the bone when it is too uncomfortable to confront. You must listen quietly for the silence of their unspoken doubts and stir up the pot of awareness and change. You must turn down the heat of anger and reduce your words until the essence of what boils is revealed. And over time, with experience, you will come to know when the seasoning is just right and a real, home-cooked friendship has been presented to your table. And then you must offer your best china, pour freely, the cream, and savor, sister, savor for "a [woman] that hath friends must shew [herself] friendly" (Prov. 18:24) and that is truly tasty, indeed.

Monique Headley

59

Dirty Rice with Shrimp

8 ounces ground beef

8 ounces smoked beef sausage, sliced

2 scallions, chopped

1 green pepper, diced

1 garlic clove, diced

2 tablespoons cooking oil

1 pound medium shrimp, peeled, deveined

1 cup beef stock

½ cup cooking sherry

½ cup Worcestershire sauce

1½ cups long grain rice, cooked

¼ teaspoon cayenne pepper

½ teaspoon paprika

½ teaspoon oregano

1 bay leaf

¼ teaspoon thyme, whole

1¾ teaspoon seasoning salt

¼ teaspoon black pepper

In a large saucepan, brown ground beef and sausage. Drain. In a separate pan, sauté scallions, green peppers, and garlic in oil. Add shrimp and cook until done. Add stock, sherry, and Worcestershire sauce and simmer. Add cooked rice, spices, and ground beef and sausage to shrimp mixture. Raise heat and stir. Cover and cook for 2 minutes. Remove from heat and let stand for 5 minutes. Remove bay leaf.

Yield: 4 Servings

Recipes for Living

"The best restaurant my kids want to eat at is mom's kitchen."

Rev. Steven Warfield
R.H. Boyd Publishing Corp.
Nashville, TN
Married 30 years

Dirty Rice with Shrimp
recipe on page 60

61

Crab Cakes

1 pound imitation crabmeat

¼ cup celery, diced

¼ cup red peppers, diced

¼ cup onion, diced

¼ cup yellow peppers, diced

¼ cup green peppers, diced

¾ cup bread crumbs

2 tablespoons mayonnaise

1 teaspoon Worcestershire sauce

Dash celery salt

Dash white pepper

Dash Cajun seasoning

¼ teaspoon paprika

Dash dried chives

¼ teaspoon dill

½ cup Parmesan

Coating

1 egg, beaten

¾ cup milk

2 cups bread crumbs

In a bowl, mix crabmeat and all other ingredients. Adjust seasoning if needed. Mix egg and milk for the coating. Scoop out crab mixture. Then roll in the egg and milk coating. Add the bread crumbs on top. Form small cake patties using hands. Place on a parchment pan. Preheat deep fryer to 350 degrees. Cook crab cakes until golden brown.

Yield: 10 servings (2 each)

Recipes for Living

"Family time is the best at dinner because we are all together and my wife's meals make it special."

Matthew Parker
President, Institute for Black Family Development
Detroit, MI
Married years

62

La Mardi Gras Chicken

Wash and dry chicken breast. In a shallow bowl, combine chicken, Italian dressing, wine, garlic, thyme, white pepper, and 1 tbsp of seasoning salt. Marinate overnight. Preheat oven to 350 degrees. Place cooking oil in a saucepan over medium heat. Place chicken in pan and blacken on both sides. Then place chicken in oven for 30 minutes to finish cooking. With remaining oil, sautee vegetables. Add 1 tablespoon of seasoning salt to the vegetables. Serve chicken topped with sauteed vegetables.

Yield: 4 servings

20	ounces skinless boneless chicken breast
1	cup Italian dressing
2	tablespoons white cooking wine
1	tablespoon minced garlic
1	tablespoon whole thyme
1	teaspoon white pepper
2	tablespoons seasoning salt
2	tablespoons cooking oil
1	green pepper, cut up
1	red pepper, cut up
1	yellow pepper, cut up
1	carrot, cut up
1	yellow onion, cut up

Recipes for Living

"It is good to come home to a woman who has excellent cooking skills."

Brendon Barclay
Atlanta, GA
Married 7 years

63

Paprika Chicken

2 green peppers
4 onions, chopped
4 celery stalks
4 tomatoes
4 pounds chicken pieces
¼ cup sour cream
1 tablespoon paprika
⅛ teaspoon salt
¼ teaspoon Worcestershire sauce
¼ cup butter
½ (10 ounce) can cream of mushroom soup
2 tablespoons cornstarch
2 tablespoons water

Prepare vegetables by cutting into very coarse pieces. Brown chicken in butter in a large skillet. Add green peppers, onions, celery, and tomatoes. Simmer, covered, for 15 minutes. Combine remaining ingredients, except cornstarch and water, in a small pan. Heat just to boiling over moderate heat, stirring occasionally. Pour sauce over chicken and vegetables. Cover and continue cooking over low heat for 1 hour. If sauce is thin, thicken with cornstarch dissolved in cold water and add as needed.

Yield: 8 Servings

Recipes for Living

"Good cooking has kept me around for a long time."

Rev. Eddie Gaffney
Pastor, Universal Community Church
Chicago, IL
Married 29 years

A Call to Order

"For God is not the author of confusion."

I Corinthians 14:33

Imagine for a second that while getting ready for work one Monday morning, you receive a phone call. It's not just any phone call, however. It is a phone call that could change your life forever. The person on the other end of the line says that you have won a most special gift. The gift is that you no longer have to work a 9 to 5. They inform you that you can live the rest of your days doing whatever you choose to do. However, in order to claim the award you must, within the next 15 minutes, fax to the number provided a copy of your personal and work-related achievements for the past 12 months.

Would you, in 15 minutes, be able to submit achievements, recommendations, reviews and other pertinent information to the caller? How excellent it would be to have your things in order at such a time. Order is light. Order is peace. Order is of God. But, oh what a time it would be to have everything in a mess! Disorder is confusion. God is not the author of confusion. Add order to your life. Arrange your stuff. If you have papers laying all over the place, apply a filing system to them. Better yet, set up a computerized filing system and scan (or type) your documents onto your computer. I once heard it said that it is better to be

prepared for an opportunity and not have one, than to have an opportunity and not be prepared for it. Being prepared means being ready to act on a moment's notice. It's having a clear path to easily step through an opened door.

God has placed everything in order. And we are to reflect His glory. Confusion and messiness do not reflect the character of God. You can take steps today to bring order to your world.

Vanessa R Salami

Peered Veal Cutlets

4 veal cutlets, thin
¼ teaspoon seasoning salt
¼ teaspoon black pepper
¼ teaspoon granulated garlic
1 egg, beaten
1 teaspoon milk
¾ cup bread crumbs, toasted
2 tablespoons vegetable oil
2 tablespoons butter
4 lemon wedges

Pound veal with a mallet to tenderize. Sprinkle cutlets with seasonings. Turn meat over in an egg and milk mixture. Then turn meat over in crumbs. Heat oil and butter in heavy pan until bubbly. Sautee meat until brown on both sides. Drain on paper towels and serve with lemon wedges.

Yield: 4 Servings

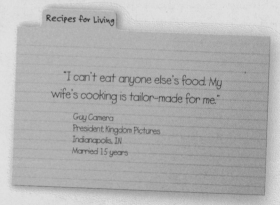

Recipes for Living

"I can't eat anyone else's food. My wife's cooking is tailor-made for me."

Guy Camera
President, Kingdom Pictures
Indianapolis, IN
Married 15 years

Red Beans & Rice

Wash and soak beans over night until swollen. Bring beans, chicken broth, and water to a boil; reduce heat. Cut sausages and brown in a skillet; remove from skillet. Add remaining juice and vegetables and cook until tender. Combine meat and cooked vegetables and all other ingredients and cook for 2 hours; add water if needed.

Yield: 8 servings

1 regular bag Camilla beans

4 cups fat-free, less-sodium chicken broth

1 cup water

1 pound beef sausage

1 package Aunadui sausage

1 cup chopped onion

1 cup chopped bell pepper

¼ teaspoon crushed red pepper

2 garlic cloves, crushed

1 cup scallions

2 bay leaves

1 tablespoon garlic Mrs. Dash

1 teaspoon cayenne pepper

1 tablespoon old bay seasoning

1 tablespoon Cheshire seasoning

Recipes for Living

"She knows what I want to eat without me asking."

Calvin Giddens
Director of Sales and Promotion, Urban Ministries, Inc.
Chicago, IL
Married 38 years

67

Shrimp Creole

- 1 can of cream of mushroom soup
- 1 tablespoon of tomato paste
- 1 can of Rotel
- 1 tablespoon of olive oil
- 1 small chopped onion
- ½ cup scallions
- 1 garlic clove, minced
- 1 teaspoon of old bay seasoning
- ½ teaspoon of garlic powder
- 1 tablespoon of Cheshire seasoning
- 1 teaspoon Worcestershire sauce
- 1 pound of peeled and deveined shrimp

Combine soup, tomato paste, and Rotel in sauce pan over low flame. Heat 1 tablespoon of olive oil and add onion, scallions, and garlic. Cook until onions are tender. Add seasonings to sauce and cook for 35 minutes over medium heat, stirring occasionally. Add shrimp and cook for 7 more minutes.

Yield: 4 Servings

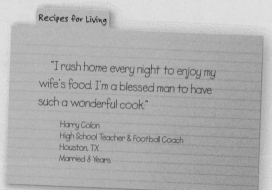

Recipes for Living

"I rush home every night to enjoy my wife's food. I'm a blessed man to have such a wonderful cook."

Harry Colon
High School Teacher & Football Coach
Houston, TX
Married 8 Years

Seafood Jambalaya

Heat oil in saucepan and sauté onions, peppers, chorizo, and shallots. Add sherry. Add rice, chicken stock, spices, and tomato sauce. Bring to a boil, then simmer until rice becomes tender. Add shrimp, oysters, and crabmeat. Simmer until shrimp is cooked. Adjust seasonings if needed and serve warm.

Yield: 6 servings

½ cup salad oil
⅔ cup onions, diced
⅔ cup green peppers, diced
1 pound chorizo, skinned and diced
¼ cup shallots, diced
¼ cup cooking sherry
3 cups rice, uncooked
1 quart chicken stock
⅔ cup parsley
Dash thyme
Dash Cajun spice
Dash seasoning salt
Dash black pepper
Dash garlic salt
1 pint tomato sauce
2 pounds shrimp, medium peel, devein
1 dozen oysters, shucked
1 pound crabmeat, squeeze dry

Recipes for Living

"As her cooking has evolved, so has our marriage."

Chris Meadows
President, Bringing Christ to the Game
Jamestown, NY
Married 8 years

Frying Family Fun

Now therefore take, I pray thee, thy weapons, thy quiver and thy bow, and go out to the field, and take me some venison; And make me savoury meat, such as I love, and bring it to me, that I may eat; that my soul may bless thee before I die." Genesis 27:3-4

These words were spoken by Isaac to Esau. Isaac was an old man with two things left to do: Bless his son with his inheritance and have his last enjoyment—some good food prepared by his family.

When there are no family jewels to pass on, there is usually a family legacy passed on through the kitchen. I'm sure you can relate to tasting something cooked just right and immediately being transported back to your family's kitchen. It's like that for me with rice pudding—Mom always made it with the leftover rice from dinner. And nothing can compare to my mom, Winnie Clark's potato salad. "The key, you know, is to dice the potatoes small." Or Aunt Edna's grape jelly, made from the grapes growing outside on the vine. I even remember the wax on top to provide the seal on the jar. Oh, it was pure joy to taste Papa Clark's "secret" barbeque sauce (Don't tell anybody, but it's equal parts mustard, ketchup, apple cider vinegar, molasses, and Worcestershire sauce).

Another family legacy is that we were always together for dinner, all eight of us. Mom at one end of the table and Papa Clark at the other. We always thanked the Lord before anything went on our plates (although I confess to scoping out which chicken leg I'd dive for when the "Amen" was over.) I chuckle when I remember the times sitting around the kitchen table laughing and telling stories. Each story was more embellished, especially when cousins Carrie and Obreen and their daughter Tanya came to visit.

Except for Aunt Edna's grape jelly, which one day I'll try, every one of those recipes are made in my own kitchen, including the recipe for laughter. Of course we've added a few legacies of our own. My husband taught all our girls to do fractions by teaching them measurements in cooking. There's nothing more precious than seeing a little girl standing on a chair, covered with flour, making cookies with her Daddy.

Mom's with the Lord now, and so is Aunt Edna. But the memory of their kitchens and the smells, tastes, and sounds found there, even the colors of their aprons, are so etched in my mind that I stopped typing this for a minute to be there in my memory once again. Now when I go home, we still always sit in the kitchen, cooking and tasting and it's not long before somebody says, "Remember the time . . . ?" and the laughter begins again.

Michele Clark Jenkins

Smoked Turkey Crepes

Begin with Hollandaise sauce: Cook egg yolks in a skillet on the stove. Remove from heat. Stir in butter, white wine, peppercorns, and parsley. Sprinkle with a dash of salt and keep warm. In another pan, heat cream until it is halfway gone – approx. 10 minutes, then place to the side. Place mushrooms in a small bowl and cover with hot water. Let stand for 1/2 hour. Drain, saving the liquid. Strain liquid through a coffee filter to remove all of the grit. Chop mushrooms. In a frying pan, heat 1 tablespoon butter. Mix in onion and garlic and cook for 5 minutes. Stir in wine and cook for 5 minutes. Add all mushrooms and cook briefly. Stir in mushroom liquid and cook for 5 minutes. Mix in smoked turkey, parsley, and reduced cream. Place crepes in a skillet and brown – approx. 1 minute each. Fill crepes with mixture and fold. Top with the hollandaise sauce

Yield: 6 Servings

½ cup whipping cream
½ cup mushrooms, sliced
1 ounce dried porcini mushrooms
½ cup wild mushrooms, sliced
  Hot water
1 tablespoons butter
¼ teaspoon garlic, minced
2 tablespoons onion, chopped
¼ cup white wine
1 cup smoked turkey, chopped
1 teaspoon parsley, chopped
12 crepes

Hollandaise
2 egg yolks
3 tablespoons butter
2 tablespoons white wine
1 teaspoons green peppercorns, cracked
¼ cup parsley, chopped
  Dash salt

71

Spicy Lime Shrimp

1 tablespoon cooking oil

½ teaspoon minced garlic

Salt and pepper to taste

1½ pounds shrimp, uncooked, peeled, deveined

1 pound linguine, cooked

2 tablespoons cilantro, chopped

Beurre Blanc

¼ cup onion, chopped

1 cup white wine

1 teaspoon lime juice

¼ teaspoon thyme, chopped

1 bay leaf

1 cup whipping cream

1 tablespoon flour

6 tablespoons butter

¼ cup tequila

Mix oil, garlic, salt, and pepper. Coat shrimp with oil mixture. Cover. Refrigerate 30 minutes. Toss linguine and cilantro. Keep warm. In a skillet mix onion, wine, lime juice, thyme, and bay leaf. Cook over high heat until mixture is reduced. Stir in cream and flour. Reduce heat to medium. Remove bay leaf. Remove mixture from heat. Slowly whisk in butter. Mix in tequila. In another pan heat shrimp and cook till there is no pink. Mix shrimp into sauce. Serve shrimp mixture over linguine.

Yield: 6 Servings

Recipes for Living

"My wife's food is more than staples and seasonings. It's a representative of good love, caring and patience."

Max Siegel, Esq.
President, Verity Records,
Vice President, Zomba Music Group, USA
New York, NY
Married 7 years

Simmering Singleness

With all of the temptations and people with alternative agendas, the new millennium is a frightening time to be a single woman. Because of the demands from society most of us have had to take on traditionally masculine roles. We work from 9 to 5, worry about bills, and fight to climb the corporate ladder.

Society has become so fast-paced that we pump our own gas and fix minor repairs on our cars and in our homes.

After all that we endure in a day, we come home to a place that lacks an encouraging smile or a comforting hug. We graciously use our feminine touches to make our homes relaxing and appealing. Yet, at some point the question inevitably arises, "Am I destined to remain single, or is there the slightest possibility that I'll be blessed with a loving husband?" In some cases there is such an urgency to make a union become reality that we convince ourselves that even the "wrong one" is right for us.

What I am beginning to realize is that God has called us to this time for a reason. Our struggles are much different from our grandmothers'. Millennium men are not the same as our grandfathers were. Our ancestors came up during a time when they had no choice but to be patient. Today's microwave society has influenced us to become people who are insistent on receiving instant gratification. We often develop the mentality that we are gods who are in total control of our destinies. We want our destiny when we want it and how we want it. God's way is much different.

God works in seed-harvest time. He cultivates the growth-yield process. He is a patient God and, if we are to be more like him, we must follow David's direction in Psalm 27:14 and "Wait on the Lord: be of good courage, and he shall strengthen thine heart: wait, I say, on the Lord." If we choose to look at our single lives as a reflection of our attempt to learn godly patience, we will become more cheerful in our waiting for the man who God is preparing for us. All the while, we must trust that God has abundant blessings in store for us. And it's completely possible that they will one day include a worthy husband who will recognize and appreciate our inner beauty and Godly strength.

Tajauna TJ Butler

Apple-Raisin Strudel
with Vanilla Rum Sauce

5 large apples peeled and sliced

1 cup ground yellow cake crumbs

1 cup raisins

½ cup rum

1 package filo dough

2 sticks of butter (melted)

Sugar

Vanilla Rum Sauce

1 cup milk

½ tablespoon vanilla

1 tablespoon corn starch

1 egg yoke

¼ cup sugar

2 tablespoons rum

Combine apples, cake crumbs, raisins, and rum and set aside. On a cutting board, lay down one sheet of filo dough, brush with melted butter and sprinkle with granulated sugar. Repeat this procedure until you have 6 sheets of dough completed. Place 2 to 3 cups of filling in a line down the center of the dough. Fold one side of the dough over the filling. Brush the edge with butter and fold the other side over it. Tuck the ends inside and place on a non-stick-baking sheet. Brush with butter and sprinkle with sugar. Bake for 45 min. at 350 or until golden brown. Cut into 2" slices and serve warm.

Mix 1/2 cup milk and vanilla in saucepan and bring to a boil. Mix 1/2 cup milk with cornstarch, egg yoke and sugar, and add to boiling mixture. Mix well. Stir constantly for 1 minute. Add rum. Remove from heat and serve warm over strudel.

Yield: 12 Servings

Crème Fruit

3 egg yolks, beaten
4 tablespoons sugar
Dash salt
1 cup milk
½ teaspoon vanilla
½ cup strawberries, halved
½ cup pineapple chunks
½ cup bananas, cubed
½ cup mandarin oranges
½ cup cantaloupe, chopped
½ cup honey dew melon, chopped

Mix egg yolks, sugar, and salt in a skillet. Stir in milk. Cook for 20 minutes. Remove sauce from heat. Stir in vanilla and cook for 1 minute. Remove from heat and let cool. Refrigerate for 1 hour. Serve over fruit.

Yield: 6 Servings

Recipes for Living

"We please each other with our cooking."

Anderson Flewellen
Owner, Mirage Photography
Atlanta, Ga.
Married 9 years

Cutting the Excuses

This recipe is a wholesome, soul-satisfying meal, rich in nutrients for strengthening your level of confidence and your ability to complete God's assignments. "I can do all things through Christ which strengtheth me" (Phil. 4:13). Cutting excuses requires a mixture of Spiritual Confidence. The following ingredients will get you started: one cup of our zesty Father, one cup of his freshly ground Son, and one cup of the soul-satisfying Holy Spirit. Each ingredient has a unique function and should be spiritually combined in a large bowl. Although you will blend the 3 together to make one batter, it is necessary to spiritually blend them so that they each maintain their spiritual uniqueness. After the ingredients have been properly blended, the next step is to prepare your heart to receive the mixture of Spiritual Confidence.

In preparing your heart, the following is required: 1) Believing in God, 2) accepting God's Son, Jesus Christ as your personal Savior, and 3) guidance of God's Holy Spirit. Preparation of the heart is an essential part of this recipe: No substitutions can be made. Once your heart has been prepared, your soul should now be heated. Pour the unique blend into your heart. Start with the Father, then the Son, and finish with the Holy Spirit. When the ingredients began to boil, reduce to simmer, stirring occasionally. For those of you who struggle with the challenge of excuses, you may need to stir more frequently. Once Spiritual Confidence has had a chance to simmer and the right nutrients and spices begin to melt into your heart, you can now CUT THE EXCUSES! Feast on the feeling of being prepared. Savor the essence of increased performance. Let the confidence of fulfilling God's purpose tantalize your taste buds.

In the body of Christ, God has blessed us with our own spices—or shall we say, spiritual gifts. Each ingredient has a unique function. Each function is imperative as a whole in the body of Christ. When we create excuses in our daily lives, the excuses seek to overwhelm God's recipe for His perfect purpose. The faith we have in the trinity; The Father, the Son, and the Holy Spirit will grant us the confidence needed to CUT THE EXCUSES! "Being confident of this very thing, that he which hath begun a good work in you will perform it until the day of Jesus Christ" (Phil.1:6).

Cathy Ann Johnson

Pecan Diamonds

Crust:
1½ sticks butter
1 cup granulated sugar
½ cup eggs
2½ cups cake flour
¼ teaspoon baking powder

Filling:
¾ pound butter
¾ pound brown sugar
½ cup granulated sugar
1 cup honey
3 ounces heavy cream
11/2 pound chopped pecans

Crust:
Cream butter and sugar until fluffy. Add eggs and then flour and baking powder. Kneed into a ball and chill for 30 minutes. Cut dough in half and roll out 1/8" thick onto a 13" x 17" piece of parchment paper. Place onto a 12 x 16½ sheet pan; use a fork to punch holes in the dough to prevent air bubbles. Bake at 350° for 20 minutes or until light brown. The remaining dough may be used to make cut-out sugar cookies.

Filling:
Bring butter, brown sugar, granulated sugar, and honey to a boil. Boil for 15 minutes and then remove from the heat. Add the cream and pecans, and place back on heat and bring to a boil, cooking for 5 more minutes. Poor filling into pre-baked crust and bake for 10 minutes at 400 degrees. Cool for 30 minutes and remove from pan. Refrigerate for 1 hour. Cut away edges. Cut 1 ½ inch strips diagonally then repeat the steps for the other side creating diamond shapes. Serve at room temperature.

Yield: 1-1/2 sheet

Praline

Combine brown sugar, granulated sugar, salt, milk, and cream of tartar. Bring to a boil and heat to 236 degrees (use a candy thermometer). Then add butter, vanilla, and pecans. Bring to a boil and heat to 220 degrees. Remove from heat; let stand for 5 minutes. Then spoon onto baking sheet using a standard kitchen tablespoon. Let cool 30 minutes and serve at room temperature.

Yield: 25 pieces

1 cup plus 2 tablespoons brown sugar

1 cup plus 2 tablespoons granulated sugar

½ teaspoon salt

¾ cup milk

⅛ teaspoon cream of tartar

3 tablespoons butter

1 teaspoon vanilla

2 cups pecan pieces

Recipes for Living

"God is still God, hallelujah is still hallelujah, wherever you are! Praise Him!

Co-Pastor Terry
Okinawa, Japan

Southern Praline Pecan Cake

Cake

2½ cups cake flour

7 ounces shortening

1 pound brown sugar

1 teaspoon salt

½ teaspoon baking powder

¼ teaspoon baking soda

½ cup buttermilk

1 teaspoon vanilla

1⅛ cup eggs

½ cup buttermilk

¼ cup chopped pecans

Praline Icing

1 pound powder sugar

1½ sticks butter

2 tablespoons water

⅔ cup brown sugar

¼ teaspoon salt

3 tablespoons evaporated milk

½ teaspoon vanilla extract

Cake

Using a paddle, cream together cake flour and shortening until smooth. Add brown sugar, salt, baking powder, baking soda, buttermilk, and vanilla to the mixture, scraping down bowl and mixing until smooth. Mix eggs, buttermilk, and pecans, and add in two parts; mix until smooth. Pour batter into 2 greased 8-inch cake pans and bake at 350 degrees for 35 minutes or until done.

Praline Icing

Place powder sugar in mixing bowl and set aside. In a saucepan, bring to a boil butter, water, sugar, and salt and heat to 238 degrees. While hot, add this mixture to powder sugar. Mix to a smooth paste. Add evaporated milk and vanilla. Beat until it is well mixed. Spread icing between the layers, on the sides, and over the top of cake.

Yield: 2 8-inch rounds

African Peanut Chicken
recipe on page 24

Samboska
recipe on page 32

82

Seafood Paella
recipe on page 34

83

Mango-Lime Cake
recipe on page 42

84

Mango-Lime Cake
(showing interior)
recipe on page 42

Minted Iced Tea
recipe on page 14

86

Honey Wheat Beer Bread
recipe on page 48

87

La Mardi Gras Chicken
recipe on page 63

88

Paprika Chicken
recipe on page 64

Shrimp Creole
recipe on page 68

91

Seafood Jambalaya
recipe on page 69

Apple-Raisin Strudel
with Vanilla Rum Sauce
recipe on page 74

93

Pumkin Bread
recipe on page 108

94

Martinique Punch
recipe on page 113

95

Curried Meatloaf
recipe on page 122

Trinidadian Spiced Chicken
recipe on page 133

Banana Fritters
recipe on page 136

Marinated Fried Chicken
recipe on page 165

Smothered Pork Chops
recipe on page 167

Southern Fried Catfish
recipe on page 168

105

Red Velvet Cake
recipe on page 176

Caribbean

recipes from the islands

Caribbean Cooking

The Caribbean is known for its beautiful islands, white sandy beaches, blue mountains, exotic fruits, and friendly people. Lying within the tropical zone, the Caribbean Islands are famous vacation spots. People of all nationalities spend time relaxing and enjoying the wonderful scenery and tasty food.

The Caribbean's most popular associations are with it's sweet tropical fruits like: pineapples, bananas, kiwi, mango, and coconuts. Nuts are plentiful and are sometimes preferred over heavy meals to enhance the mental peace of the beautiful surroundings. As with many traditions, the recipes have been improved and adapted to fit new surroundings.

The history of the foods of the Caribbean goes back to our dear mother Africa, where very spicy foods are so popular. Jamaica is very famous for jerk chicken; it is both spicy and sweet.

The "jerk" cooking process involves grilling or roasting the meat and then adding a special seasoning mix. Vegetables are even jerked. If you can not handle spicy food, this dish is not for you! Unlike other spicy dishes, deletion of the chili pepper vastly changes the end product.

Caribbean meals are very tasty, colorful, and masterfully designed. The ability to incorporate tropical fruit into main dishes is truly an art in itself. The blending of sweet and spicy palates allows the meal to be filling and light all at once. Caribbean cooking closely its African heritage by using rice as one of its staples.

Desserts from the Caribbean revel in the large variety of tropical fruits and nuts. You can go wild with recipes like a light and easy banana pie served with different sauces and coulis. Or you can keep it simple, serving fried bananas with a little nutmeg syrup.

Float

Soak yeast in ¼ cup water for 10 minutes. Add remaining water, sugar, salt, shortening, and flour. Beat well for 10 minutes. Kneed on well-floured surface. Place back in bowl, brush top with butter, cover with a damp cloth and let rise until double in size. Shape into small balls and let rise again. Roll out into thin round circles and fry in hot oil until golden brown.

Serve with fried shark or ham.

½ package dry yeast
¾ cup warm water
1 teaspoon sugar
3 tablespoons butter or shortening
3½ cups cake flour

Recipes for Living

"A good meal is the final product of an organized day."

Nicole Smith
Kindergarten Teacher
Phoenix, AZ

Pumpkin Bread

2 cups cake flour
4 cups wheat flour
1½ teaspoons baking soda
1 teaspoon nutmeg
1½ teaspoons cinnamon
4½ cups sugar
1 pound raisins
1 cup water
1½ cups salad oil
3 cups mashed pumpkin
6 eggs
1½ teaspoon salt

Combine dry ingredients in mixing bowl and mix for 1 minute on 1st speed. Add raisins and mix. Add water, oil and pumpkin. Mix on medium speed for 3 minutes. Add eggs slowly and mix for 1 minute. Pour batter into two well-greased 6" loaf pans and bake at 325 degrees for 50 minutes or until done.

Yield: 2 2½-pound loaves

Recipes for Living

"The only time curling up with a good book is more satisfying than a good meal is when the book is the Bible. The Word of God is some good eating."

Linda Peavy
Acting Publisher
Judson Press
Valley Forge, PA

Pumpkin Bread
recipe on page 108

Honey Pain Bread

2 packages dry yeast
1½ cups water, warm
   (110–115 degrees)
¼ cup honey
2 tablespoons oil
1 teaspoon salt
¾ teaspoon nutmeg
4 cups flour
2 tablespoons milk
½ teaspoon coffee

Mix yeast with water until creamy. Stir in honey, oil, salt, nutmeg, and 2 cups of the flour. Beat till smooth. Add remaining flour to make dough stiff. Knead until smooth. Place in a greased bowl. Turn dough upside down in bowl. Cover and put in a warm place for an hour. Make squares or rolls and put on a greased pan. Cover and let rise for 30 minutes. Preheat oven 350 degrees. Dissolve coffee in milk. Brush over the dough. Bake for 30 to 40 minutes.

Yield: 10 Servings (2 pieces each)

Recipes for Living

"By taking time to plan my meals, they are low in fat and sensible on portions which is much better for my family."

Sheryl Washington
Sales Representative, Central South Christian Distribution
Nashville, TN

Beating the Pounds

I was very thin as a young girl. They called me "Skinny." The people in my community liked to see girls with "meat on their bones." So, after years of enduring the taunts about my skinny legs, I decided to do something about it. I was on a mission to put on the pounds. I ate twice as much of the wrong things. If it was full of fat, I ate it. I devoured ice cream, Snickers bars, and lots of double cheeseburgers. There were no "Biggie" fries back then, so I'd order two large fries. Then the pounds came and so did the compliments. However, I didn't feel the way I used to feel. I was lethargic and knew deep inside that I was not being true to myself.

We are "fearfully and wonderfully made" (Ps. 139:14). The human body is one of God's masterpieces. He designed our bodies to work to the best of their abilities so that we can be our best for him. I decided one day that the extra pounds had to go, even if I had to beat them off. I gave up the delicious (but fattening) food and began to exercise. Now I realize that a healthy diet and exercise are what's best for the temple that God gave me.

(1 Cor. 6:19). Aerobic activity at least three times per week fights disease, burns fat, relieves tension, and clears the mind. I can beat those pounds off before they can jump back. Now God gets the glory instead of the pounds.

If I miss a day of exercise, I can hear the pounds giggling and laughing as they jump on my hips and thighs. But they scream in agony as I beat them off with every foot stride on the treadmill. They cry out in pain as I pump them away with weights. And I love to hear the moans and groans when I can zip up my favorite skirt again.

Montrie Rucker Adams

Ginger Beer

1 pound, 4 oz ginger washed and peeled
1 cup lime juice
1 cup lemon juice
Sugar to taste
2½ quarts cold water
1 cup soda water

Grate roots. Put into a jar and set in the sun for one day.
Mix lime juice, lemon Juice, sugar, water, and soda water.
Strain Roots. Pour mixture and root juice into a pitcher.
Put into refrigerator for 2 days.

Yield: 8 oz

Recipes for Living

"When I left my job as Essence Editor-in-chief, my eight-year-old daughter asked me 'Does this mean you, me and Dad will all sit down and have dinner as a family? And will it happen before the sun goes down?' I delighted in telling her yes! Now I'm experimenting with quick, easy dinner recipes that complement the breakfast menus I've perfected for my bed and breakfast guests at Akwaaba Mansion and Akwaaba by the Sea."

Monique Greenwood,
Entrepreneur, author and former editor, Essence Magazine
New York, NY

Martinique Punch

Mix all ingredients into a punch bowl and stir.
Garnish with the lemon and orange slices.

Yield: 8 Servings

2 liters ginger ale
1 can pineapple juice
1 can orange juice, frozen
1 can lemonade, frozen
1 cup grenadine
½ cup sugar
1 lemon, sliced
1 orange, sliced

Recipes for Living

"I'm not a great cook at all. However, I've learned that to
make my life the best it can be, I have to take care of my family.
So, after much prayer and practice I don't burn every dish
anymore. Nothing makes me feel better than having my husband
tell me how delicious my meal is. And if it's real good, he serves
me the rest of the evening."

Stephanie Perry Moore,
Author of the Payton Skky Series & Flame and the Editorial Director for Nia
Publishing. Atlanta, GA

Sea Moss Drink

¼ cup Sea moss

2 quarts water

1 lime

⅓ Angostura bitters 2 cups milk

Sugar to taste

Rinse off sea moss. Place sea moss in pot with 2 quarts of water and the juice of one lime. Boil for 45 min. Whip in a blender until mixture looks like milk. Add bitters, milk and sugar. Serve with crushed ice.

Yield: 8 oz sea moss

Recipes for Living

"Just as eating from different food groups is necessary to stay healthy, so is combining a variety of spiritual disciplines—Bible study, prayer, and fellowship— necessary to live a balanced, godly life."

Laryssa Toomer
Homemaker/Writer & Speaker
Fayetteville, NC

Chayote Rice

Heat 2 teaspoons oil in a skillet. Add chayote and cook for 5 minutes. Remove chayote. Then mix into the skillet onion, garlic, and the remaining oil. Stir in rice. Cook for 8 minutes. Stir in chayote, tomato, salt and pepper. Let simmer. Sprinkle with chives.

Yield: 6 Servings

3 tablespoons oil
1 chayote, pared and cut into ½ in pieces
1 onion, chopped
2 garlic cloves, chopped
4 cups rice, cooked
1 tomato, chopped
¼ teaspoon salt
  Dash pepper
  Dash chives

Recipes for Living

Beholding with joy the pleasure
    Exhibited through your child's look
As with satisfaction he or she measures
    The meal you lovingly cooked
Making worth while the daily hustle and bustle
    As you view the approval on your child's face
Gladdens your soul deeply, with joy unspeakable
    Strengthening you to continue to run a woman's hectic pace

Richelle Hollie Guillory
Author: **The Known Stranger** (a murder mystery); **Expressions of Soul**
(a compilation of original poetry); and **Articles of Inspiration**
(a compilation of inspirational articles for spiritual refreshment)
Inglewood, CA

Wiping Away Tears

The loss of a relative or loved one is one of the most difficult things for us to face. We all experience a sense of loss and fear. To make it through this time of trial, we must have a clear understanding that God is in control of all things, at all times. Whatever it is that has happened, God could have prevented it if he had chosen to. We also need to know that God does not use death as a means to punish us or hurt us.

God often brings us in to bring us out. There are some lessons that only adversity can teach us. In the book of Genesis we read about how Joseph was placed in a pit by his brothers and forgotten in prison by his friends, only to discover that what man meant for evil, God meant for good. Joseph withstood unfair treatment, heartache, and sorrow at the hands of those who loved him, yet he remained faithful (Gen. 50:20). The more weight the champion weightlifter lifts in practice, the more he can lift in the competition. God has prepared you for every adversity that comes in your life.

Finally, Revelation 7:17 says "And God shall wipe away all tears from their eyes." What a wonderful consolation that the God of the universe, the maker of heaven and earth, shall comfort us once and for all!

Tears will always be a part of our life on earth, death and sorrow is something we cannot escape. Tears should remind us of the joy of heaven. When God shall wipe away all our tears, we will be completely healed of all our sorrow. It is only then that we will truly be free of all anxiety, grief, and pain. Beloved, rest assured that God shall wipe away all of your tears!

Jarnell Meeks

Curacao Fruit

Toss fruit and liqueur.
Refrigerate for at least 1 hour.

Yield: 6 Servings

½ cup s halve
½ cup wh pes, seedless
½ cup pineapple chunks
½ cup bananas, cubed
½ cup mandarin oranges
½ cup cantaloupe, chopped
½ cup green apples, chopped
½ cup melon, chopped
3 tbsp orange-flavored liqueur

Recipes for Living

"Maneuvering through life means dressing out of a suitcase and eating out of a bag. But this traveling mentality makes you mindful to pack your knee pads. You've got to stay prayed up to make it."

Marlow Shields-Talton
T.D. Jakes Ministries
Cedar Crest, TX

Haitian Rice

1 onion, chopped

2 garlic cloves, minced

1 green pepper, chopped

2 tablespoons cooking oil

1 cup rice, uncooked

4 ounces ham, cooked, and diced

2 cans (15 ounces each) kidney beans, drained

½ teaspoon cumin

¼ teaspoon salt

¼ teaspoon oregano

¼ red pepper, chopped

2½ cups water, boiling

Preheat 350 degrees. Cook and stir onion, garlic, and green pepper in oil. Combine this mixture and the remaining ingredients and pour into an ungreased baking dish. Cover and cook in the oven for 1 hour.

Portions: 6 Servings

Recipes for Living

"Maintain the balance of good food and good nutrition for children. Then their little hearts and minds will be ready to serve Jesus."

Jean Alicia Elster
Children's book author
Detroit, Michigan

Peas and Rice Curry

Separate peas by rinsing them in cold water. Drain. Heat oil and butter in a skillet. Mix in onion, curry powder, and salt. Add peas and rice. Simmer for 8 minutes.

Yield: 6 Servings

1 cup rice, cooked
1 tablespoon oil
1 tablespoon butter
1 onion, chopped
1 teaspoon curry powder
¼ teaspoon salt
1 package (10 ounces) green peas, frozen

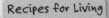

Recipes for Living

"Eating well is all about respect for the vessel. When the system is well fueled, mind and soul are better able to focus on everything else. Eat well, live faithfully and prosper!"

Monique Headley
Manager of A&R, Verity Records/Zomba Gospel Publishing
New York, NY

119

Curried Shrimp

1 pound large shrimp, deveined

2 tablespoons lemon juice

¼ teaspoon garlic, granulated

¼ teaspoon onion salt

2 tablespoons vegetable oil

1 medium onion, chopped

½ cup chopped green peppers

2 tablespoons curry powder

½ cup cream

2 cups rice, cooked

Sprinkle raisins

Dash shredded coconut

Place shrimp in a bowl. Combine lemon juice, garlic, and onion salt and coat the shrimp with it. Let stand for 10 minutes. Heat oil in a large skillet. Sauté onions and peppers. Pour in curry powder. Add cream slowly. Stir and simmer until mixture thickens — approx 15 minutes. Add shrimp. Cook for 15 minutes on low. Serve over rice. Garnish with raisins and coconut. Serve hot.

Yield: 4 Servings

Recipes for Living

"In the midst of a busy day, I make time for a proper lunch. It makes me much more productive."

Sharon Payne
Owner, Bronzeville Living Word Bookstore
Chicago, IL

Curried Shrimp
recipe on page 120

121

Curried Meat Loaf

1 pound ground beef

1 egg, beaten

1½ teaspoon curry powder

1 cup toasted bread crumbs

1½ teaspoon turmeric

1 teaspoon salt

½ teaspoon pepper

Sauce

½ cup onion (finely diced)

2 tablespoons coconut flakes

½ tablespoon ground ginger

1 tablespoon lemon juice

4 ounces curry paste

1 tablespoon oil

Preheat oven 350 degrees. In a bowl, mix together all ingredients until smooth. Form the meat mixture into a loaf and place into a loaf pan. Bake at 350 degrees for 45 minutes.

Sauce

In sauce pan, sauté onions. Add the other ingredients and simmer at low heat. Serve on top of the meat loaf.

Yield: 4-6 Servings

Recipes for Living

"It's hard getting a balance, but a strong prayer life and a heathly meal manage to give me balance in the midst of the struggle."

Chrystal Gaines
Manager, The Harvest Bookstore
Lindenworld, NJ

Mixing in Checkups

Ladies. Even though your day may be busy, it is imperative that you don't forget to take care of yourselves physically. Remember your bodies are the temple of God. "For ye are the temple of the living God" (2 Cor. 6:16). A classic body-saving jewel begins with remembering to eat a well balanced diet and exercise regularly 20 minutes a day. The second gem is preventative medicine. This is important to detect and alter risk factors for diseases such as increased cholesterol, pre-symptomatic states as for cervical cancer, and pre-clinical stages as for breast cancer. Here are some suggestions to encourage you to include regular check-ups into your busy schedule.

With breast cancer being the second leading cause of cancer death in women, lifetime risk is estimated at 1 in 8 women. African-American women are at highest risk and mortality from breast cancer. Check-ups for women should routinely include a clinical breast examination. After age 40 women should have a mammogram every 1 to 3 years, and every year after 50 to 55 years old.

Cervical cancer is another reason to schedule an annual pause in a hectic year. The American Cancer Society estimated that at least 12,800 new cases and 4,800 deaths occur each year from cervical cancer. Risk factors for cervical cancer are early age onset of sexual activity, multiple sexual partners, a history of sexually transmitted disease, and smoking. It is recommended that screening begin with the onset of sexual activity or age 18 years old, and every 1-3 years, thereafter, depending on individual risk accessment. Therefore, check-ups should include getting annual pap smears for screening of cervical cancer.

Another important health screen is for colon cancer. The lifetime risk of developing colon cancer is a relatively low 6%. 90% of colon cancer occurs in individuals greater than 50 years old. Tests used for detection are fecal occult blood test, proctoscopy, flexible sigmoidoscopy, barium enema, and colonoscopy. Annual fecal occult blood tests decrease mortality by 30%.

Up-to-date immunizations are important. Immunization is one of the greatest successes of modern medicine for preventing disease and for extending life. Adults need immunizations throughout life. These include measles, rubella, tetanus, diptheria, hepatitis A & B, influenza, rabies, pneumococal. Please contact your primary care provider for further details.

Other important check-up concerns are blood pressure, cholesterol, smoking and HIV status. Please take time out of your busy day, and mix in a check up. "He was wounded for our transgressions, he was bruised for iniquities: the chastisement of our peace was upon him; and with his stripes we are healed" (Is. 53:5).

Taiwanna Brown-Bolds

Chicken Plantain & Pineapple Skewers

8 chicken breasts, boneless, skinless

4 bacon strips (cut in 1½ inch pieces)

½ pineapple peeled, cored, and cut into chunks

2 ripe plantains, peeled and cut into chunks

½ cup pineapple juice

¼ cup lime juice

2 tablespoons oregano, chopped

2 garlic cloves minced

½ cup oil

Pineapple Dipping Juice

2 tablespoons oil

1 onion, minced

10 ounces pineapple fruit spread

Using 8 or 10 inch skewers, alternately thread chicken, bacon, pineapple, and plantains. Place skewers in a shallow tray or glass baking dish. Mix pineapple juice, lime juice, oregano, and garlic. Coat the skewers with the marinade, saving the extra marinade. Wrap tray and refrigerate for 45 minutes. Preserve marinade by brushing skewers lightly with oil. Place chicken on preheated grill and cook for 20 minutes, turning often. Serve with Pineapple Dipping Sauce.

Pineapple Dipping Juice
In sauce pan heat oil and sauté onion. Add pineapple fruit spread and reserved marinade. Bring to boil, stirring often until thickened.

Yield: 4 Servings

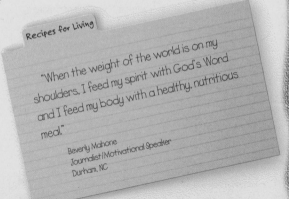

Recipes for Living

"When the weight of the world is on my shoulders, I feed my spirit with God's Word and I feed my body with a healthy, nutritious meal."

Beverly Mahone
Journalist/Motivational Speaker
Durham, NC

Citrus Roast

Preheat oven to 325 degrees. Place roast in a bowl. Mix 1 cup orange juice and lime juice. Pour over roast. Cover and refrigerate for at least 3 hours. Remove pork from juice. Reserve juice. With a paper towel dry the pork roast. Mix garlic, oregano, and pepper. Rub over pork. Place onion, celery and carrot in a pan. Sprinkle this mixture with salt. Pour reserved juice over the vegetables. Put pork roast on top of the vegetables. Cook roast in the oven and bake for 2 hours or until done. Serve hot.

3 pounds pork roast, boneless
1½ cups orange juice
¼ cup lime juice
3 garlic cloves, minced
1 teaspoon oregano
½ teaspoon pepper
1 onion, diced
½ cup celery, sliced
1 carrot, sliced
1 teaspoon salt

Yield: 8 Servings

Recipes for Living

"I make a plan and I set goals. After that, I just stick to it. I've found that you must stay committed to whatever you say you're going to do."

Patrice Baker
Representative, Bill Winston Ministries
Oak Park, IL

Jamaican Beef

3 pounds boneless rump beef roast

½ pound Italian sausage

2 tablespoons oil

3 garlic cloves, minced

2 bay leaves

1 onion, chopped

1 green pepper, chopped

1 teaspoon oregano

1 teaspoon salt

¼ pepper, chopped

1 can (8 ounces) tomato sauce

Cut a hole in the middle of the beef roast. Fill the hole with Italian sausage. Heat oil in skillet until hot. Cook beef in oil for 15 minutes. Drain excess fat. Add remaining ingredients. Bring to a boil. Reduce heat. Cover and simmer until beef is tender. Cook for 2 hours.

Yield: 8 Servings

Recipes for Living

"It takes discipline to stay organized and plan balanced meals."

Shun Naylor
Owner, In Faith Christian Bookstore
Raleigh, NC

Jamaican Papayas

Cook and stir beef, onion, and garlic in skillet until beef is brown. Drain. Stir in tomatoes, jalapeno peppers, salt, and pepper. Simmer for 10 minutes. Preheat oven to 350 degrees. Scoop mixture into each papaya half. Sprinkle with cheese. Place all 8 in a baking dish. Pour a little water into the bottom of the pan. Cook uncovered for 30 minutes.

Yield: 4 Servings

1 pound ground beef
1 onion, chopped
1 garlic clove, minced
1 can (16 ounce) tomatoes, whole, drained, and cut
1 jalapeno pepper, minced
½ teaspoon salt
¼ pepper, chopped
4 papayas, halved and seedless
2 tablespoons Parmesan cheese

Recipes for Living

"I have to make time to fix myself good food, but I've found that I am worth the extra effort."

Ruby Wheeler
Owner: Globe Bible Bookstore
Detroit, MI

Pork Casserole

1½ pounds pork, boneless and cubed

1 onion, chopped

¼ cup vinegar

3 bacon slices

¼ teaspoon red pepper

2 cups hot water

1 cup rice, uncooked

2 teaspoons parsley

¼ cup olives

1½ teaspoon salt

Preheat oven to 350 degrees. Mix pork, vinegar, onion, garlic and red pepper in a bowl. Cover and refrigerate for at least 4 hours. Fry bacon until crisp. Drain grease. Take pork out of marinade. Reserve marinade. Cook and stir pork in bacon fat until pork is totally browned. Drain. Mix pork, reserved marinade, bacon, and remaining ingredients in an ungreased casserole dish. Cover and cook at 350 degrees for 30 minutes.

Yield: 4 Servings

Recipes for Living

"It is beautiful to know that after working long past 8 hours a day, God blesses my body with an abundance of food just as he blesses my soul with an abundance of faith."

Sonnie Beverly
Author
Atlanta, GA

Spicy Fried Codfish

Boil fish in water on the stove. Reduce heat. Cover and simmer for 5 minutes. Drain. Sauté onions in cooking oil. Preheat deep fryer. Mix remaining ingredients until smooth. Stir in fish. Stir in onions. Drop mixture into the deep fryer. Fry until golden brown.

Yield: 6 Servings

6 cod fillets
2 onions, chopped
2 tablespoons oil
1 cup flour
1 egg, beaten
3/4 cup milk
1 teaspoon baking powder
1 teaspoon salt
1 teaspoon oil
1/4 teaspoon pepper

Recipes for Living

"Whatever your goals are, whatever you want to do in life, like Nike says, 'Just do it.' Lay out a plan then follow it month by month, week by week and day by day until the goal is accomplished."

Laundria Perriman
Equestrian Rider
Miami, FL

Stirring Up Success

I know a lot of people who would describe themselves as successful. I have heard many even boast, "Everything I touch turns to gold." Often they run thriving businesses, drive luxury cars, live in the best neighborhoods, take fabulous vacations, and dress in the best clothes.

Most people who fit the above description work hard, really hard. And, most of them are really good at and passionate about what they do. They go to success seminars and they know all of the motivational "slang" to get themselves and their staffs pumped up for higher performance.

There are many Christians who fit into this group. Some of them have adopted the world's formula for success. They have put success above all things, even God. Often unknowingly, they find they take have God out of their work lives and ignored the priorities he set for them. They attempt to live a life out of order before a God of order.

Many don't make it home to dinner with their families because there is just one more piece to put into the deal. They may develop an ulcer or any number of other stress-related illnesses, because they are so concerned about making as much money as they can to keep up a certain standard of living.

It is typical that choices they have made and their ungodly priorities begin to produce fruit from the seed they have sown and their lives begin to unravel. Unless there is a change, the seed planted will always bear its own fruit.

True and lasting success comes to those who confess Jesus as their Lord and Savior and order their lives on the promises of God. How do we know if our success is the kind of success that God talks about or if it is the success the world brings?

Easy. Look at your fruit.

How is your life going? Do you seem to go from victory to victory or from tragedy to tragedy? Does God's anointed, yoke destroying, burden-removing power show up at your point of need, or are you still trapped in past sadness, pain, bitterness, and unforgiveness? Do you have peace?

True success for Christians is more than just "things." God wants to give us the desires of our hearts but what he wants first is for our hearts to desire him. Seeking the kingdom of God is to seek God's way of doing things. Our personal relationship with God must be the most important thing in the world to us. Next should be our spouses, then our children, and finally, our jobs or ministries.

We can fool ourselves into believing that God is the most important thing in our lives—until something happens. Then we run around trying to get a bank loan or find a miracle cure or someone we met a long time ago who would surely know how to help us out of our dilemma.

God knows.

And he also knows our hearts—even better than we do. When we order our lives the way God tells us to—we do not have to seek out success. Godly success seeks out us!

How do we learn more about God's priorities and about the success from him that will hunt us down? Do we have to go to expensive seminars? Scream loud affirmations? Read lots of books? Nope.

Only one Book. God's Book. The Bible has a life success plan laid out specifically for each of us. Yet each begins the same, "But seek ye first the kingdom of God, and his righteousness; and all these things shall be added unto you" (Matthew 6:33).

Denise Stinson

Tomato Chopped Ham

4 ounces ham, cooked and chopped

1 onion, chopped

2 garlic cloves, minced

1 jalapeno pepper

2 tablespoons oil

1 can (16 ounce) tomatoes, whole and chopped

2 tablespoons parsley

1 teaspoon vinegar

⅛ teaspoon pepper

2 cans (14 ounce each) hearts of palm, rinsed and sliced

Parmesan cheese

Mix onion, garlic, jalapeno pepper, and ham in a bowl. Heat oil in a skillet. Add mixture to skillet once hot. Cook and stir for 5 minutes. Add tomatoes, parsley, vinegar, and pepper. Bring to a boil. Reduce heat. Simmer uncovered until mix is thick. Add hearts of palm. Cover and simmer for 5 minutes.

Sprinkle with cheese before serving.

Yield: 6 Servings

Recipes for Living

"I started getting more into cooking in college. I missed the good, home-cooked meals my mom prepared at home and decided that it was time to start making my own. Besides, cooking helps me watch my eating habits. Now I prefer yesterday's cream of mushroom baked chicken over a hamburger any day."

Nicole Duncan,
2001 graduate University of Alabama
Tuscaloosa, AL

Trinidadian Spiced Chicken

Preheat oven 350 degrees. In bowl mix chicken, oil, and spices. Place seasoned chicken on parchment-lined sheet pan. Bake for 30-35 minutes or until chicken is done. Cool chicken and slice it length-wise. In bowl, mix chicken with red peppers, red onions, cucumbers, and pineapples, and toss in dressing. Serve immediately.

Dressing
In a food processor add all ingredients and pulse until pureed.

Yield: 6 Servings

6 chicken breast, boneless, skinless
2 tablespoons vegetable oil
1 teaspoon garlic, minced
2 teaspoons curry powder
1 tablespoon crushed red pepper
1 teaspoon paprika
½ teaspoon thyme, whole
1 red pepper, diced
½ cup red onion, minced
1 cucumber, diced
1½ cup pineapple, diced

Dressing
3 tablespoons olive oil
¼ cup fresh lime juice
1 cup parsley
¼ cup chopped chives
2 tablespoons thyme leaves
½ teaspoon salt
¼ teaspoon pepper

133

Baking with Faith

I have always enjoyed baking. It seems to soothe my spirit and bring peace. There is something about beating cake batter or shaping cookies or fluting a piecrust that is beautiful and calming.

When I was working in corporate America, I would come home after a day filled with racial discrimination and sexual innuendoes and bake a cake. I would create something beautiful and delicious and thereby renew my faith in the beauty of life and humankind. I even remember a high school student who sent me a note that read, "Mrs. Kimbrough, I need a chocolate chip cookie!" Of course, I baked her some. I knew that whatever was distressing her would be quieted by the delicious taste and texture of the cookies. In fact, my children always encouraged me to open a bakery.

I suppose that I have always imagined that God is a great cook. He must consider each human being according to a marvelously spectacular recipe. When he has assembled all of the ingredients and baked that person to just the right color and texture, he sets that person free to move and work in the world. That act of setting humans free demonstrates God's faith in us and in his creation. What we do with our ingredients is up to us. God did not make us robots without control of our lives. We are free to choose and to serve and to make the most of who we are. We can stand by and let our ingredients dry up, or we can keep them moist and active. It's an act of faith both by us and by God. Let us try not to disappoint him. Bake with faith!

Marjorie L. Kimbrough

West Indian Stew

Heat chicken, water, and bullion in a skillet Bring to a boil. Reduce heat. Cover and simmer for 15 minutes. Add remaining ingredients except for the chives. Bring to a boil again. Reduce heat. Cover and simmer until chicken is done. Garnish with chives.

Yield: 8 Servings

Recipes for Living

"No matter how good the food we don't eat the whole pot; likewise with great projects, we can't do the whole lot."

Sabrina D. Black
Founder and Clinical Director of Abundant
Life Counseling Center
Detroit, Michigan

3 pounds chicken, boneless, skinless (cut up)

6 cups water

2 tablespoons beef bouillon

2 tomatoes, chopped

2 onions, diced

2 potatoes, cut into ½-inch slices

2 sweet potatoes, cut into ½-inch slices

2 cans corn

1 squash, chopped

½ cup green peas

1 hot chilis, stemmed and sliced

2 tsp salt

¼ teaspoon pepper

Dash chives

Banana Fritters

1 cup cake flour

Salt to taste

2 teaspoons baking powder

2 tablespoons sugar

3/4 teaspoon cinnamon

1 egg

1/2 cup milk

1 tablespoon melted butter

2 cups mashed bananas sprinkled with lemon juice

Sift dry ingredients. Whip egg and add milk and butter to it. Add liquid to dry ingredients. Beat one minute. Add bananas. Drop by tablespoons into hot oil. Fry to a golden brown color. Dust with powder sugar and serve warm.

Portions: 4 servings

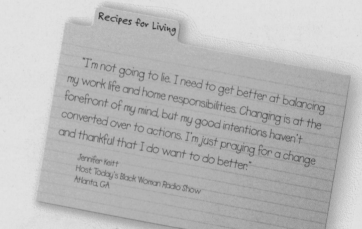

Recipes for Living

"I'm not going to lie. I need to get better at balancing my work life and home responsibilities. Changing is at the forefront of my mind, but my good intentions haven't converted over to actions. I'm just praying for a change and thankful that I do want to do better."

Jennifer Keitt
Host, Today's Black Woman Radio Show
Atlanta, GA

Lemon-Lime Meringue Pie

Crust

Cream butter and sugar; then add egg. Add flour and baking powder and blend well. Chill for 30 minutes. Roll out to 1/8"x 11" circle and place in pie pan.

Filling

Cook custard powder, water, and cornstarch until thick. Remove from heat and add margarine, sugar, yokes, and rinds. Add lemon and lime juice. Pour into crust.

Meringue

Whip whites on high speed for one minute. Slowly add sugar, vanilla, and lemon juice. Whip until it forms a peak. Place on top of filling and bake for 45 minutes at 350 degrees. Refrigerate one hour. Serve cold.

Yield: 1 9-inch pie

Crust

- 3/4 stick butter, softened
- 1/2 cup sugar
- 1 egg
- 1 1/4 cups cake flour
- 1/4 teaspoon baking powder

Filling

- 4 tablespoons custard powder
- 1/4 cup water
- 1 1/2 tablespoons cornstarch
- 2 ounces margarine
- 4 ounces sugar
- 2 egg yokes
- 2 lemon rinds
- 2 lime rinds
  Juice of 2 lemons & 2 limes

Meringue

- 2 egg whites
- 1/4 cup sugar
- 1 tbsp Vanilla extract and lime juice to taste

Mini Banana Pies

Crust

- ³/4 stick butter, softened
- ½ cup sugar
- 1 egg
- 1¼ cup cake flour
- ¼ teaspoon baking powder

Filling

- 5 cut up bananas
- 1 cup sugar
- ¼ cup rum
- 8 ounces crushed pineapple, pureed
- 2 tbsp apricot glaze

Crust

Cream sugar and butter; then add eggs. Add flour and baking powder and mix well. Chill 30 minutes. Make small balls and roll out to ⅛" x 2½" circles. Place on a non-stick baking sheet and bake for 22 minutes at 350 degrees. Let cool.

Filling

Cook bananas, sugar, and rum in a saucepan. Bring to a boil then remove from heat. Drain liquid from bananas. Spoon ¼ cup onto each circle and brush with melted apricot glaze. Serve pureed pineapples on the side.

Rum Bread Pudding

Mix together bread, coconut, cherries, and raisins, and pour into a 9-inch square pan. Mix milk, eggs, sugar, rum, and spices, and pour over bread mixture. Let soak for 30 minutes, and then bake at 350 for 1 hour or until done.

Yield: 1 9-inch square casserole dish

1 loaf white bread, broken into small pieces

½ cup coconut

½ cup maraschino cherries (diced)

½ cup raisins

2 cups milk

2 eggs beaten

4 cups sugar

½ cup rum

Vanilla, cinnamon, and nutmeg to taste.

Recipes for Living

"Find something to stand for or fall for anything .. . Play the cards that you're .... dealt ... Shoot for the moon and fall amongst the stars.... these are my favorite quotes that like good food fill me up and keep me going."

Carla McGhee
Women's National Basketball Association, Orlando Miracle and member of the 1996 USA Gold Medal Basketball team.
Orlando, FL

Pouring Tithes

Having been raised a good Catholic girl, the concept if tithing seemed an impossible act. I recall being forced to church each Sunday as children, our mighty obligatory donation envelopes in hand. We were dollar Christians for sure. Our Sunday donation, along with our monthly tuition fees, would surely help build the kingdom of God. On very cold Sunday afternoons and most times on warm spring Sunday afternoons, too, we donated a large portion of our kingdom-building funds to the local bodega (market) and obtained a hefty assortment of the most forbidden fruit.

What did God need with our money? I assumed God had nothing to do with money since it always seemed that many Christians were broke or nearly broke. Too many of us prayed on Sunday, hollering for deliverance after we had lost the mortgage at the blackjack table Saturday night. God seemed to allow the enemy to oppress us Monday through Friday, as we struggled to make ends meet. One step away from the "shut off" notice, we were expected to donate to the less fortunate. The church was filled with the "less fortunate." God did not need my money. If God needed me to give him some of my money, he should've helped me make it.

After recently becoming a Baptist, my pastor spoke on the subject of tithing. I was ignorant to Malachi 3:8-10: "Will a man rob God? Yet ye have robbed me. But ye say, Wherein have we robbed thee? In tithes and offerings. Ye are cursed with a curse: for ye have robbed me, even this whole nation. Bring ye all the tithes into the storehouse, that there may be meat in mine house, and

prove me now herewith, saith the Lord of hosts, if I will not open you the windows of heaven, and pour you out a blessing, that there shall not be room enough to receive it." I tried to reason with this passage. I still didn't know what God needed with money and food. What caught my attention was the promise God makes. God is eternal. God's plan for us is an eternal promise for an abundant life made before the time of our conception. There is no limit or timeframe when God makes a promise. God's promise in return for our tithing is a huge blessing, a blessing so large it pours out through the windows.

The concept of tithing is more important than the material benefits. The church should have material benefit from our tithes. All will benefit from the spiritual gifts of tithing. When we tithe a small portion of our income, we are practicing faith. God rewards faith and obedience with blessings. I am reminded of 1 Samuel 15:22, where we are told that obedience is better than a sacrifice. God does not require our material offering. He requires our obedience to his commands. In obeying his commands, we are acting on faith. God, our Father, is aware of our needs, desires, and sacrifices. "Faith is the substance of things hoped for, the evidence of things not seen" (Heb. 11:1).

The reward for our faith may not be visibly apparent, but God knows the desire of our hearts. I am a tithing member of my church. I make a material sacrifice each Sunday. I do not care if the deaconate and pulpit sport the finest furs, wear jewels, and drive luxury sedans. God is aware of my needs and has met them all. I do not allow the distractions of material wealth or envy to get in the way of my being obedient with a glad heart. I pray the church leadership will do God's will, not their own, with my sacrifice.

I was obedient to the call of an additional offering for the building fund. I wrestled with the idea for a month. When my heart was glad, I rushed to add my donation to the building fund. The fund would help make repairs on the parsonage. Although my own home was in need of many repairs, I was obedient and glad to answer the call. God made

continued on pg. 142

continued from pg. 141

a way and opened windows. I applied for, and surpris-
ingly received a grant from the county to make repairs
on my own home. God blessed us in a large way.

God has made a way for me, since I've made room
for God. God has allowed me to work from home for
the past three years. I am able to be creative in my own
space. My life has been returned to my children and me.
Any working mother knows the heartache of leaving a
baby with a sitter while she works to make everyone else
rich. I resentfully worked an exhausting job during three
pregnancies. I left my babies behind while I struggled to
keep my head above water. Thank you, Lord. I am now
equipped with the tools to supply my needs and God will
meet me with peace of mind.

Otilia Tanner

soul

recipes that combine art of cooking with the love of God

Soul Food Cooking

"Soul food" is a term used to describe the style of cooking created by the African slaves in the southeastern United States. Ingredients such as beans, fresh fruits, wild game, starchy vegetables, as well as old tribal customs, became the dietary customs still practiced today. One misconception regarding soul food is that slaves ate the parts of the pig the masters did not want because they had no choice. The origins of pork dishes are in Africa, where eating the walls of the pig's stomach is a dish called "tripe," cooked with pig tails, pig feet, onions, cayenne pepper, and tomato sauce, and served family-style with fufu.

Another popular dish with African origins is African flat bread which is prepared similar to hot cakes, although hot cakes are eaten with sweet syrup and flat bread is served warm with soup.

Many soul food dishes came about when the slave cooks had to cook dishes that their masters requested of them. Utilizing the resources available, and their knowl-

edge of cooking, they created soul food. In addition to cooking in the master's house, they created meals for their own families, using even fewer resources. relying on their customs from home, they not only created awesome dishes, but the love and care they placed in the cooking process allowed their spirits to be free in spite of their enslaved bodies. They remembered the old ways of home and how cooking was sacred, and the way the family was thought of through the cooking process. They applied this simple system to their condition, which seemed hopeless, and kept their families sharing and laughing despite their challenges.

Recently soul food cooking has come under heavy criticism because of its fat content. The key to soul food cooking is not just how flavorful and fattening the food is, but rather the ability of the cook to allow the love and anointing of God to flow through them. As you prepare your dish, remember that it is not how much fat you use, but rather the wisdom of the true art, comfort, and love of soul food cooking.

Cheese Biscuits

Preheat oven to 500 degrees. Mix all ingredients quickly with as little handling as possible. Roll thin. Cut with cookie cutter to make round patties. Bake in the oven for 10 minutes.

Yield: 6 servings

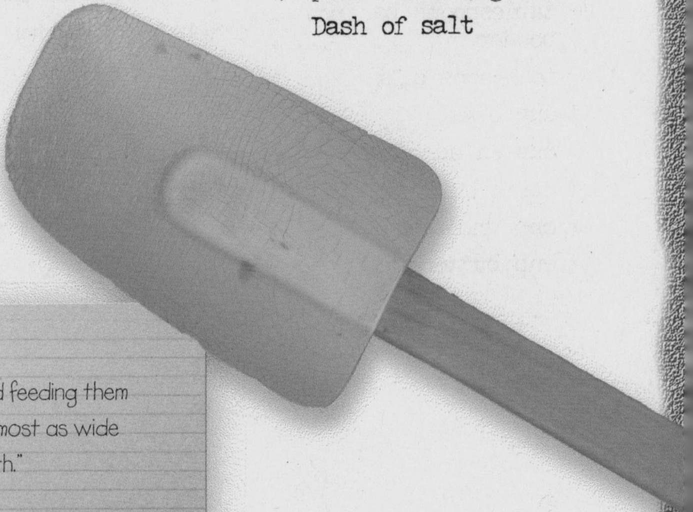

½ cup flour
¼ pound butter
3 tablespoons ice water
¼ pound cheese, grated
   Dash of salt

Recipes for Living

"Keeping my grands and feeding them puts a smile on my face almost as wide as the sky spans the earth."

Hazel Randall
Ettrick, VA
Grandmother of 2

Fried Corn Bread

2½ cups self-rising corn meal

3 cups cake flour

2 cups sugar

1½ tablespoons baking powder

½ teaspoons salt

1 cup eggs

½ cup salad oil

¼ stick butter, melted

¾ cup whole milk

¾ cup buttermilk

Combine dry ingredients and mix well. Add eggs, oil, and melted butter. Mix well. Add milk and buttermilk. Mix well. Heat a cast iron skillet on stove until very hot. Add oil to cover bottom of pan. Pour batter into the hot pan, covering the bottom. Let fry until bread is light brown on bottom and done throughout the middle. Serve hot.

Recipes for Living

"I've always been accustomed to preparing mammoth portions of food when cooking for my large family of 11 children. Now that they are all grown and scattered about, my hands find it difficult to prepare smaller portions."

Armealie Lee
Louisville, Kentucky
Grandmother of many

Blending Happiness into Everything

You are some happy women when everything is going great in your lives. Your man is acting like the man of God you thought you married. Your clients are paying you on time, which means the bills are being paid on time. The kids are acting like they've got some home training, and you've managed to keep you weight down for the past few years. You look good, you feel good, and you're just fabulous!

The challenge is maintaining that state of great delight and contentment when all hell breaks loose and you can't see God anywhere in sight. The man is acting like he's demon possessed—he left with an unsaved woman 15 years his junior. Your clients haven't paid you on time in 5 months and your home has gone into foreclosure. The kids decide that they all want to go crazy at the same time. The stress is so great, you've lost track of your eating and exercise regimen and your weight is up 30 pounds. You ask yourself, "How am I to feel any kind of joy, contentment or happiness?" You think that no one can possibly have joy with all this mess going on.

True, it is extremely difficult to blend happiness into everything under these circumstances, but it is possible to exercise contentment under whatever circumstances we face. When we learn to be content and endure whatever state we find ourselves in when we continue to press forward, we soon find ourselves passed the place where we were and on to better things, as we see the hand of God move in our lives in miraculous ways. Knowing this, that the trying of your faith worketh patience." (James 1:3) From patience comes character, and character hope. The love of Christ is our hope and he is faithful to honor his promises and complete the good work he began in us.

"Behold we count them happy which endure. Ye heard of the patience of Job, and have seen the end of the Lord; that the Lord is very pitiful, and of tender mercy" (James 5:11).

As we all know, Job literally lost everything. But in the end God restored, resurrected, and put things back together for Job and he was blessed far above what he lost. Learn to encourage yourself and blend contentment with faith when things are not going well. Exercise your faith by believing God has a plan for your life no matter how it looks or feels.

Dina Ruth Andrews

Down Home Punch

       juice
1 cu   ge juice
½ cup lemon juice
1 cup pineapple juice
1 cup water
1 cup sugar
    Zest from 1 lemon
1 bottle maraschino
    cherries, drained, and
    cut into pieces
1 quart ginger ale

Combine fruit juices. Boil water, sugar, and lemon rind together for
5 minutes. Strain and let cool. Then add cherries.
Refrigerate for 1 hour.
Add ginger ale before serving.

Yield: 8 servings

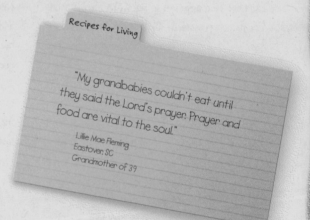

Recipes for Living

"My grandbabies couldn't eat until
they said the Lord's prayer. Prayer and
food are vital to the soul."

Lillie Mae Fleming
Eastover, SC
Grandmother of 39

Teacolade Punch

Pour ingredients into a bowl.
Stir for 2 minutes.

Yield: 10 servings

1 quart sweet tea
1 quart lemonade
2 liters cola

Recipes for Living

"As pure as the snow is around my
house, that is just how pure my heart is
to put my all into feeding my
grandchildren."

Ms. Dixon
Flint, MI
Grandmother of 4

Alabama Cheese Grits

2½ cups milk
¾ cup grits, uncooked
½ cup butter
½ tsp salt
⅓ cup Parmesan cheese
1 (5 ounce) jar sharp cheese spread

Preheat oven for 350 degrees. Bring milk to a boil.
Add grits and cook for about 10 minutes. Stir in butter, salt, and cheese. Spoon into a lightly greased baking dish.
Bake for 20 minutes.

Yield: 6 servings

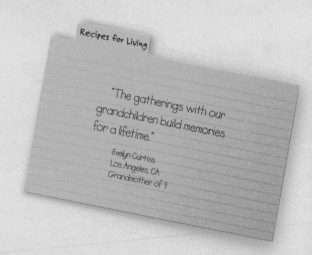

Recipes for Living

"The gatherings with our grandchildren build memories for a lifetime."

Evelyn Curtiss
Los Angeles, CA
Grandmother of 9

Baked Cheesey Macaroni

Preheat the oven to 375°. Boil the macaroni and drain. Pour macaroni in large baking dish. Mix in the seasoning salt and black pepper. Next, mix in the butter, eggs, cream of mushroom soup, and cheddar and mozzarella cheeses. Mix well; pour in the milk and place in the oven. Cook, uncovered, for approximately 25 minutes, or until light brown on the top.

Yield: 8 servings

Macaroni (Large bag)

2 eggs

1 ½ cup of milk

1 stick I Can't Believe It's Not Butter (sliced)

1 cup Cheddar cheese (shredded)

1 cup Mozzarella cheese (shredded)

Can of cream of mushroom soup (Campbell's preferably)

Seasoning salt (to taste)

Black Pepper (to taste)

Recipes for Living

"Cooking doesn't take much smarts. Good cooking takes a lot of love and an unselfish heart."

Catherine Ross
Columbus, OH
Grandmother of 6

Egg Rolls

2 eggs
1 ounce cake yeast
5 cups bread flour
1 teaspoon salt
½ cup sugar
¼ cup MALT
¼ cup oil
2 cups cold water

Whip 1 egg to a froth. Break up yeast and add to mixture. Add flour, salt, sugar, malt, water and oil. Mix for 15 minutes or until developed. Kneed dough on a well-floured surface; cover and let rise until dough has doubled in size. Cut into small balls and let rise again doubling in size. Whip up one-egg and brush rolls with egg wash. Bake at 400 degrees or until golden brown.

Recipes for Living

"The one thing that used to keep us as a black family together was the fact that we ate dinner together. It kept us close and united. The old saying, 'The family that eats together stays together,' still rings true."

Candi Staton
Stone Mountain, GA
Grandmother of 17

Sautéing Self Time

It's time to put the sizzle back in your lives ladies! If your life has become rote, boring, stale, lifeless, frustrating or hectic; non-stop, constantly-moving-ninety-miles-per-hour-without-a-break—then I'm talking to you. Girl, it's time to put the zest, zing and meaning back into your life again by indulging in some much needed self-time!

Self-time is the process of rejuvenating and letting go of the woman we were yesterday and are, even today, to become the women God wants us to be! "But they that wait upon the LORD shall renew their strength; they shall mount up with wings as eagles; they shall run, and not be weary; and they shall walk, and not faint." (Is. 40:31). I don't know about you, but I am so ready to have renewed strength! (Just call me Super Woman!) I'm ready to soar with the eagles, run and not grow weary in my well doing, and walk my life out without wanting to give up, cave in or quit! How about you, are you ready? Good, now let's find out how.

Scripture is clear that a key component in self-time is waiting on God's time! He is the re-newer of our strength! We must realize, ladies, that creating a sizzling self-time requires taking care of the total you: spirit, soul, and body! It's pampering and nurturing, feeding and empowering your spirit through prayer, meditation, and feeding on God's word daily. It's cleansing and organizing your mind and emotions through journaling, taking walks and sorting through the "junk" thoughts, feelings, and emotions that keep us burdened down. Self-time is also body time! Don't forget your diet and exercise. Please love you enough to get annual pap smears, mammograms, dental check-ups and beauty shop time! If we would make our self-time—spirit, soul and body—a major priority, we would slowly, but surely, find our way out of darkness and into God's marvelous light with lives worth living! Sautéing self-time—cook it up today!

Jennifer Keitt

Fruited Coleslaw

1½ cups shredded cabbage
½ cup apples, chopped
2 tablespoons raisins
¼ cup pineapple chucks, drained
1½ teaspoon celery seed
½ teaspoon mustard
¼ cup mayonnaise
1 tablespoon lemon juice
½ cup sugar

Combine the cabbage, apple, raisins and pineapple. Set aside. Combine remaining ingredients and mix well. Pour mixture over cabbage and stir. Chill for 2 hours.

Yield: 2 servings

Recipes for Living

"Planning a balanced meal for your family, consisting of fresh fruits and vegetables is important...after all, You Are What You Eat."

Hazel C. Fain
Silver Spring, MD
Grandmother of 2

Mustard Greens

Take about tablespoons of vegetable oil, chopped onions, and the turkey necks and pour them into a pot. Add the seasoning salt, black pepper, and garlic powder. Sauté on medium heat for about a half a minute. Pour three cups of water into the pot and then place the greens in the pot and turn heat to high. Allow the greens to settle in the pot for a while. Give about three or five mild shakes of hot sauce, or to taste. Mix in the clove of minced garlic and ½ stick of margarine. Let cook until desired consistency. You're ready for the greens of your life!

Yield: 8 servings

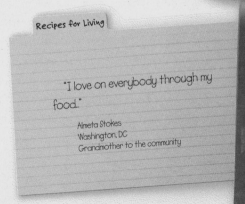

Recipes for Living

"I love on everybody through my food.."

Almeta Stokes
Washington, DC
Grandmother to the community

2 tablespoons vegetable oil

One medium size onion, chopped

2 smoked turkey necks

Lawry's Seasoning Salt (to taste)

Black pepper (to taste)

Garlic powder (to taste)

3 cups water

6 bushels of mustard greens

Hot sauce (Louisiana Hot Sauce preferred)

1 clove of garlic, minced

½ stick of margarine

Boiling High Praise

"My soul shall be satisfied as with marrow and fatness; and my mouth shall praise thee with joyful lips" (Psalm 63:5).

"Thou hast turned for me my mourning into dancing; thou hast put off my sackcloth, and girded me with gladness" (Psalm 30:11).

Girl, if you were freezing cold what would you choose to eat or drink? I'm sure it would not be ice cream. You would probably choose something delicious and hot. You might dream of a bowl of hot soup, a cup of hot chocolate, or hot tea. You might even imagine a bowl of hot spicy chili to warm your cold bones. Think about it. Ain't nothing like a big bowl of homemade chicken soup when Old Man Flu has got you down.

Well my sista, there is nothing like a hot cup of cider on a cold winter's night and there is nothing like getting your praise on during the coldest time in your life. Absolutely nothing compares to the feeling that you get while giving God all the praise. Just throw your hands up, tap your feet, rock from side to side, run down the aisle, or do whatever the Spirit leads you to do. Let me tell you the very best thing about Boiling High Praise. You don't have to save Boiling High Praise for a special occasion. Boiling High Praise can be served any and every day. Honey, I dare you to get your praise on in the car on the day that you started to call in sick. Get your praise on while fixing that meal that's everyone's favorite except yours. Try Boiling High Praise in the bathroom just before you put on that last bit of eye shadow. God loves the attention and I'm sure it will make you feel better, too. There is one important thing that you must remember—Lukewarm Praise just doesn't work. Lukewarm Praise is like lukewarm coffee—you may start drinking it, but you are sure to put it down. Girl, I think that part of your problem is that you have put your praise down.

I've been telling you to come visit my church, my pastor is teaching us how to "Praise the Hell out of Yourself." Don't you laugh—you really can praise the hell out of yourself. He broke it down and told us that praise is the dessert to your meal. If you've never listened to me before, please listen now. A hot serving of peach cobbler after a big meal is great, but there's nothing like

Boiling High Praise after being fed the Holy Word. If you're worried about wrinkling your Anne Klein suit or messing up that 80 dollar perm you got on Saturday, then Boiling High Praise is not for you. But, if you are interested in watching God show up and show out, then you just might want to jot down this recipe for Boiling High Praise. First remember to use only the freshest ingredients. You will need:

2 cup grace
1 cup mercy
3 teaspoons hope
2¾ cups the Word
1 pinch of faith

Combine all of these ingredients and bring to a boil. Cover with peace and serve immediately. Choose your favorite garnishes, but I suggest these: a sprinkling of shabach or barach.

I am sure that once you have had a taste of Boiling High Praise, you will never add any doubts or fears to your recipe again. You will never be tempted to put a pinch of jealously into your meal again. This is a recipe that you will not want to keep as a family secret. Instead you'll want to share it for generations to come. Remember that when the blessings go up, the praises come back down. So, girl, the next party that you have, have it for Jesus and invite him to share a bowl of Boiling High praise with you. If you have never experienced Boiling High Praise, then you have never had a full-course meal. Girl, I've got to go—I think I feel a Praise coming on!!

Hallelujah!

Robin M. Dial

Potato Salad

7 large eggs (chopped)

12 medium-size potatoes

Celery (about five medium size sticks, chopped)

Green onion (chopped, as many as desired)

Seasoning salt (to taste; Lawry's preferably)

Black pepper (to taste)

Garlic powder (1½ tablespoons, or to taste)

2 tablespoons of relish

1 tablespoon of mustard

½ cup of Miracle Whip (or to your preference)

Vinegar (optional; 1 tablespoon)

Boil the eggs. Boil potatoes until they've reached your desired consistency. (I boil my potatoes with the skin on them and then I take the skin off after they have boiled. I find it easier.) Stick a fork in the potato to ensure that it is done. Peel the potatoes and cut them in cubes (or as desired). Mix the eggs, celery, green onions, seasoning salt, black pepper, garlic powder, relish, mustard, Miracle Whip, and optional vinegar to desired consistency.

Yield: 8 servings

Scalloped Sweet Potatoes

Preheat oven for 350 degrees. Peel and dice the potatoes. Drop in boiling water and allow them to parboil about 15 minutes. Drain the potatoes. Dust with salt. Add butter, cream, cinnamon, brown sugar, and vanilla. Place in a baking dish. Bake for 20 minutes.

Yield: 6 servings

6 sweet potatoes
Salt
1 tablespoon butter
¼ cup cream
1 teaspoon cinnamon
¼ cup brown sugar
½ teaspoon vanilla

Recipes for Living

"My family loves my dishes and I thank the Lord, daily that he helps me prepare great meals."

Lucille Johnson Walker
Columbus, Ohio
Grandmother of 8

Virginia Spiced Apples

1 tablespoon cooking oil

½ teaspoon cloves, ground

4 apples, peeled, cored, sliced

2 tablespoons orange marmalade

Combine cooking oil and cloves in a medium bowl. Add apples. Stir well. Fry apples covered in a skillet for 10 minutes. Stir occasionally. Remove cover and add marmalade. Continue cooking uncovered for 5 minutes.

Yield: 4 Servings

Recipes for Living

"Cooking the foods that my grandchildren enjoy, sometimes prepared with their help always gives me a warm feeling of love. When we are apart and I prepare those same foods, I can almost feel their presence in the kitchen. Cooking is one of God's gifts and the smiles and laughter it brings from your family shows that you have shared that gift with people who are important to you. James 1:17: "Every good and perfect gift is from above.""

Daphne Brewington
Tampa, FL
Grandmother of 3

BBQ Pork Ribs

Preheat oven for 350 degrees. In small bowl combine spices and cooking oil. Rub mixture on the ribs. Bake for 30 minutes. In a bowl mix BBQ sauce, Worcestershire sauce, relish, and crushed red pepper. Dip ribs in sauce. Coat well. Place back into oven and cook for at least ten more minutes.

Yield: 10 servings

4 pounds pork ribs
1 tablespoon seasoning salt
1 teaspoon ground pepper
1 tablespoon garlic, minced
1 teaspoon thyme, whole
1 teaspoon cooking oil

Sauce:
2 cups BBQ sauce
1 tablespoon Worcestershire sauce
1 teaspoon pickle relish
1 teaspoon red pepper, crushed

Cleansing the Mind

THE GIRLFRIEND-TO-GIRLFRIEND RECIPE

Girl, what is this I hear about you giving up—saying that you can't do what you hoped and planned to do? You can do anything you put your mind to and handle anything God gives you. My momma used to always say "Can't never could do nothing!" and she was so right.

So many times we tell ourselves that something can't be done. We let others tell us that we can't do it and begin to believe that we really can't. But in our hearts we know that we truly can. Scripture states in Proverbs 23:7 "For as he thinketh in his heart, so is he." Don't you give up on dreams and possibilities that God intended for you to pursue. How do you really know what can be done if you don't make an assertive effort to do it? Girlfriend, cleanse your mind of negativity. Surround yourself with positive people. Let go of those people that say you can't, as well as those that don't tell you that you can. Remember negativity can sometimes show up in costume. If someone is not for you, then he or she is against you. Life is definitely too short to allow your own insecurities and un-believers to keep you from pursuing your dreams.

So what? You're laid off from work, your husband's only income is part-time, the mortgage is due, the kids need new shoes, and the family's only car is broken down. Believe me when I say that a negative approach will not help the situation. Look around, Ms. Thing—you can bet there is someone out there that has it worse than you. Not that you should thrive on this realization, because misery should not love company. Know that God takes care of His own and understand that things really could be worse.

Today is the day that you worried about yesterday. So tell me, is it really that bad? Be positive. Keep on living, believing, and trusting that things will get better and know that dreams do come true. Give God the glory, because when prayers go up, blessings do come down.

Chandra Dixon

Buttermilk Pancakes

Combine flour, baking soda, sugar and salt. Combine egg, buttermilk, and oil. Slowly stir into dry ingredients. For each pancake, pour about ¼ cup batter onto a hot, lightly greased skillet. Turn pancake when tops bubble up. And edges are browned. Serve with syrup.

Yield: 4 (2 each) servings

1 cup flour
1 teaspoon baking soda
1 tablespoon sugar
½ teaspoon salt
1 egg
1 cup buttermilk
1 tablespoon cooking oil

Recipes for Living

"I cook from the soul. It does my heart good when I see my grandbabies enjoy it."

Ann Redding
Albany, GA
Grandmother of 8

Chitterlings

1 can chitterlings
Dash salt
Dash pepper
Dash hot sauce

Wash chitterlings well. Season with salt and pepper.
Boil on stove for 1 hour.
Serve with a dash of hot sauce.

Yield: 4 servings

Recipes for Living

"If you have great cooking skills your grandkids will use it against you. They make ya cook all the time. Grandmomma can you fix me this...grandmomma can you fix me that. But ya know I love it." (smile)

Eva Shields
Dallas, TX
Grandmother of 9 (This is a black teasing quote. We know she isn't serious. Keep)

Marinated
Fried Chicken

Mix egg and milk in a bowl. Add spices. Coat chicken and marinate in refrigerator for 1 hour. Make seasoned flour by mixing flour and spices, and coat chicken with it. Heat oil in a large skillet. Cook chicken in oil for 15 minutes on each side. Reduce heat and cook for 20 minutes. Turn over once or twice until crisp.

Yield: 6 servings

1 egg
½ cup milk
1 teaspoon paprika
½ teaspoon garlic, granulated
1 tablespoon chicken bake
½ teaspoon seasoning salt
½ teaspoon white pepper
¼ teaspoon poultry seasoning
¼ teaspoon thyme, ground
3 pounds chicken, boiler-fryer cut-up
¼ teaspoon cooking oil

Seasoned Flour
½ cup flour
Dash paprika
Dash garlic, granulated
Dash chicken base
Dash seasoning salt
Dash pepper
Dash poultry seasoning
Dash thyme, ground

Recipes for Living

Cubed Steak

1 cup flour
¼ teaspoon seasoning salt
¼ teaspoon garlic salt
¼ teaspoon pepper
1 pd cubed steak
1 onion, chopped
½ cup water

Combine flour, seasoning salt, garlic salt, and pepper. Toss meat with this mixture. Brown cubed steak and onions in the skillet. Pour in water and boil. Reduce heat.
Cover and simmer for 20 minutes. Serve over yellow rice.

Yield: 4 servings

Recipes for Living

"The best thing I can do is plant seeds of righteousness, joy, and prayer, that they blossom into what God has created and predestined them to be."

Dina Andrews
Valinda, CA
Grandmother of 3

Smothered Pork Chops

Mix spices all together. Coat pork chops with spices and let stand overnight. Dredge pork chops in flour until well coated (saved left-over flour for gravy). Heat oil in large pan over high heat. Cook until brown on both sides. Remove chops from pan. Discard 2/3 of oil from pan and sauté onion and peppers. Add leftover flour and form a paste. Add water and stir until smooth. Reduce heat. Return pork chops to pan and simmer for 30 minutes.

4 pork chops
1½ teaspoons seasoning salt
1 pound ground beef
1 teaspoon dried basil
1 teaspoon oregano
½ teaspoon thyme, whole
¼ teaspoon rosemary, crumbled
2 teaspoons garlic, granulated
½ cup flour
½ cup cooking oil
½ cup onions, sliced
½ cup green peppers
1½ cups water

Southern Fried Catfish

2 eggs
¾ cup buttermilk
1 teaspoon paprika
½ teaspoon garlic, granulated
1 tablespoon seasoning salt
½ teaspoon pepper
½ teaspoon thyme, ground
6 catfish, headless, skinless
¼ teaspoon cooking oil

Seasoned Meal
½ cup yellow corn meal
½ cup flour
Dash paprika
Dash seasoning salt
Dash pepper
Dash thyme

Mix eggs and buttermilk. Add spices and stir. Coat fish with the mixture. To make the seasoned meal, mix meal and flour with spices. Coat fish with seasoned meal. Heat cooking oil in a skillet. Add fish. Cook until fish is golden brown on each side.

Yield: 6 servings

Recipes for Living

"My grandkids say that my cooking really makes them smile."

Frances E. Jefferson
Regional Administrator, Women's Bureau, Region VIII
Grandmother of 7

Marinating In Confidence

Have you ever been overwhelmed with trying to figure out how things were going to work out in your life? Will I ever find Mr. Right? Is it too late to go back to school? Can I start my own business? How will I pay the bills? How will I take care of the children? You know the syndrome. We all experience it on a fairly regular basis—it is called FEAR! Every time there is an opportunity, there is also a risk. Usually we are excited about the promotion, the challenge, the new relationship, or the move. It's the unknowns that drive us crazy with over-analyzing and anxiety. So what do you do? You marinate in confidence!

When we marinate food, we let it sit for a while. This ensures that the seasoning is absorbed by the food, which of course makes it tender and tasty. Your life is the same way. Sometimes,

you need to sit for a while and absorb what life is giving you. Let the different spices of life make you tender. Think of each challenge as a spice that is seasoning you. Don't panic, just marinate!

Remember that you are not alone. Your creator just wants you to be confident in HIM. "I can do all things through Christ, which strengtheneth me" (Phil. 4:13)! Your confidence should come from knowing that if you have the strength to survive whatever situation life has given you, you have the power to succeed. "I have been young, and now am old; yet have I not seen the righteous forsaken, nor his seed begging bread" (Ps. 37:25). When life becomes overwhelming—marinate for a while. Let the promises of God sink in and watch him turn you into a seasoned blessing for oth-

7-Up Pound Cake

3½ cups cake flour
3 cups sugar
½ teaspoon salt
1½ sticks butter, softened
½ cup oil
¼ cup shortening
½ cup 7-Up
½ cup buttermilk
5 eggs
½ tablespoon vanilla

Combine dry ingredients and mix well. Add butter, oil, shortening, 7-Up, and buttermilk. Beat mixture until fluffy. Add eggs and vanilla slowly. Mix well but do not over mix. Pour into a well-greased bundt pan or loaf pan and bake at 325 degrees for 1 hour or until done.

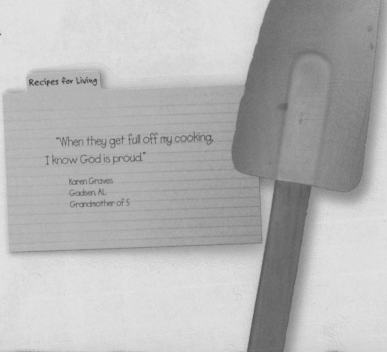

Recipes for Living

"When they get full off my cooking,
I know God is proud."

Karen Graves
Gadsen, AL
Grandmother of 5

Double Crust Apple-Walnut Cobbler

Filling:

Bring to a boil apple juice, butter, cinnamon, sugar, and vanilla. Dilute cornstarch in cold water until it looks like paste. Add to boiling mixture. Let boil until mixture is shiny. Remove from heat and add sliced apples and walnuts.

Crust:

Combine flour, sugar, and butter in bowl and mix well. Add buttermilk and mix well. Do not over mix. On a well-floured surface, roll out enough dough to cover the bottom of a 9" square baking pan about 1/8" thick. Pre-bake until golden brown at 350 degrees. Add filling 3/4 from the top of pan. Roll out remaining dough 1/8" thickness and cut strips about 1½" wide. Arrange strips across filling, spacing them 1/4" apart diagonally. Brush with butter and repeat the same procedure only going in the opposite direction creating a lattice effect. Brush with butter and sprinkle with sugar. Bake at 350 degrees until top is golden brown in color. Serve warm.

Filling:

- 5 pounds sliced apples
- 3 pounds butter
- Juice from apples
- 1 tablespoon cinnamon
- 1 tablespoon vanilla
- 8 ounces corn starch
- ½ cup cold water
- 2 cups sugar
- 2 cups chopped toasted walnuts

Crust:

- 2½ cup self-rising flour
- ¼ cup sugar
- 1½ stick soft butter
- ¾ cup buttermilk
- 2 tsbp melted butter

Homemade Banana Pudding

Custard:

- 2 cups milk
- ½ cup sugar
- 1½ teaspoon cornstarch
- 1 cup milk
- ½ cup sugar
- ⅓ cup cake flour
- 4 yokes
- 2 tspb BUTTER
- 3 cups Vanilla wafers
- 5 Bananas sliced

Custard:

Bring the milk and sugar to a boil. Combine the cornstarch, milk, sugar, cake flour, and yokes in a large mixing bowl and mix well. Add two cups of the boiling milk and sugar to the cold mixture, stirring constantly. Add all of the warm mixture to the hot mixture and continue to cook until mixture begins to thicken. Stir constantly to prevent scorching. Remove from the heat and add butter until the butter is completely dissolved. Let cool.

Using a clear glass dish, cover the bottom with vanilla wafers. Cover the wafers completely with custard. Peel and slice bananas covering the custard. Repeat this procedure until the dish is ¾ full. Chill and serve.

Optional: Cover the entire top of pudding dish with Cool Whip topping. Serve cold.

Recipes for Living

"If my grands want to eat it . . .
I'll give it to them."

Mazie L. Knight
Mobile, AL
Grandmother of 8

Proving Your Worth

Just like with you and me, the lives of the children of Israel were in deep trouble before they came to know Jehovah. Scripture compares them to an orphan that was left in a field alone to die. They were headed in a disastrous direction as a nation until Jehovah rescued them. But then God declared:

"Thus wast thou decked with gold and silver; and thy raiment was of fine linen, and silk, and broidered work; thou didst eat fine flour, and honey, and oil: and thou wast exceeding beautiful, and thou didst prosper into a kingdom" (Ezek. 16:13).

God took unloved orphans and not only gave them a home, but also a new name and the love of a holy Father. Likewise, Satan lured us into a lifestyle of sin and shame and then discarded us on the street corner with all of the baggage that we had accumulated. But the Lord has loved us anyway, despite ourselves, and entered into a covenant with us. Then He did something that superceded our expectations: He prospered us into a kingdom! The King of kings did that for you and me! He gave us the clothes of dignity and hope. He discarded the rags that we so proudly wore and replace them with royal wear fit for queens. Just that He saved us was quite enough, but now He has done more than that. In His grace, He has established us as royalty and allowed us to reign with Him. In His grace He chose to bless us with more. In biblical days, not everybody wore silk, bracelets, and embroidered cloth. Only those people who had been established as royal figures could aspire to wear such fine linens. Christ has given us a new life and a status of kings and queens. He gets so much joy in knowing that we have accepted His gift and His kindness to us and that we intend to live in a way that matches up with that gift!

Unfortunately, many women don't realize how blessed we are. We, like the children of Israel, reject what we have been given and live in rebellion. We don't appreciate all that God has done for us and therefore we squander the great inheritance that has been bestowed on us. The Jewish people did the same and as a result they spent many years unable to realize their true potential. Yet, God stood by, time and time again, and waited for His chosen people to return to Him, He waited for them to put back on the clothes of royalty that they had been granted and he encouraged them to live victoriously.

Today, God stands near waiting for you to receive the status of royalty that He is presenting to you on a silver platter. The background you have, the culture you come from, the money you make, the education you squandered, and the sins you have committed are irrelevant to Him. He stands ready to robe us in the clothes of royalty that He has had for us all along. Then, finally we can walk forward with our heads held high into our destiny.

Priscilla Evans Shirer

Ma Ma's 'Tato Pie

3 eggs

1½ cups sugar

1 cup butter

2 cooked sweet potaotes, mashed

½ cup shredded coconut

1 teaspoon lemon zest

½ teaspoon allspice

1 teaspoon vanilla

½ teaspoon nutmeg

½ teaspoon salt

1 cup milk

1 unbaked 9-inch pie shell

Preheat oven 350 degrees. Beat eggs, sugar, and butter together in a bowl until creamy. Stir in the sweet potatoes and coconut, then flavorings and spices. Add milk and beat for 3 minutes. Bake for 30 minutes in the pie shell.

Recipes for Living

"When you are called by God to do a work, it matters much to have the love and support of your mother. And it does help that she is the best cook in the world!"

Elder Marykaye Jacquet
Charleston, WV

174

Old Fashioned Carrot Cake

Mix dry ingredients. Add oil and mix well. Add carrots and pineapples and mix well. Add eggs slowly; mix well. Do not over mix. Pour into greased pans and bake at 350 degrees for 50 minutes or until done. Let cool and ice with cream cheese icing.

Cream Cheese Icing:
Cream cheese, butter, and vanilla; scrape down bowl and mix again. Add powder sugar and beat until smooth. Add walnuts. Slice the cake into layers and place icing between layers and on out side of cake. Use a little toasted nuts to garnish sides of cake.

Yield: 2 8-inch rounds

Cake:
- 2 cups cake flour
- 2 cups sugar
- 1 ⅛ tablespoon+ ⅛ teaspoon baking soda
- ¼ teaspoon salt
- 1 teaspoon cinnamon
- 1½ cups oil
- 4 eggs
- 1½ cups grated carrots
- ⅛ cups crushed pineapples (drained)

Cream Cheese Icing
- 16 ounces cream cheese, softened
- ½ stick butter
- 1 teaspoon vanilla
- 1¼ cup powder sugar
- ½ cup toasted and chopped walnuts

Red Velvet Cake

Cake:

- 3½ cups cake flour
- 3 cups sugar
- 3 tablespoons cocoa
- 2½ teaspoons baking soda
- 2 teaspoons salt
- 2 cups buttermilk
- 1 tablespoons vinegar
- 7 tablespoons red food coloring
- 2 sticks butter, softened
- 4 eggs
- 2 tablespoons vanilla

Cream Cheese Icing:

- 16 ounces cream cheese, softened
- ½ stick butter
- 1 teaspoon vanilla
- 1 ¼ cup powder sugar
- ½ cup toasted and chopped walnuts

Cake:

Combine dry ingredients and mix well. Combine buttermilk, vinegar, and color together and add to above mixture, along with the soft butter. Beat until fluffy. Add eggs and vanilla slowly. Mix well. Do not over mix. Pour into greased pans and bake at 350 for 40 minutes.

Cream Cheese Icing:

Cream cheese, butter, and vanilla; scrape down bowl and mix again. Add powder sugar and beat until smooth. Add walnuts. Slice the cake into layers and place icing between layers and on out side of cake. Use a little toasted nuts to garnish sides of cake.

Yield: 2 8-inch rounds

Recipes for Living

"I compare my grandchildren and my relationship with them to the ingredients used to make a cake, a spiritual cake. Me desire is to pour into them those traits/ those ingredients that produce an acceptable child of God. With correct amounts of sugar, kisses, sweetness, and kindness, I see them learning to love self and others."

Betty Clark
Salisbury, NC
Grandmother of 2

Sifting In Knowledge

Regardless of how one intends to prepare a meal, the task of sifting is a significant start. Whether the process requires that the tiny uncooked black-eyed peas be scanned meticulously with the naked eye and massaged ever so slightly with the brush of one's fingertip, or that the fresh, dark leaves of the collards be pulled apart and surveyed from the top of their tough stems to the bottom, sifting is necessary to screen out the valuable or nutritious crops from the unsavory or inedible.

We understand then, that to sift—to study or to investigate thoroughly—is just as vital in our walk with Christ. As children, we are blessed with the curiosity and energy to absorb all knowledge that is ours to obtain, both in our basic or academic lives, and as Christians. The peace in knowing that "I can do all things through Christ which strengtheneth me" (Phil. 4:13) is a very comforting first lesson on the life-long syllabus of Godliness.

The road to academic excellence begins and ends with commitment and a determination that regardless of the challenges, the pages of Scripture will be absorbed, marked in, folded, memorized, and understood. Once the subject matter has been mastered, we move on to even more pertinent reading, with a more scholarly mandate:

To enter the Kingdom of God.

For we realize, as Christian scholars, we must sift our way through this edification process. We must touch with reverence, ever so gently, the spiritual nutrients that are necessary for our sustenance, and remove those elements that are not. We must pull apart and tear off the leaves of unrighteousness and remain true to our course of study, with a renewed faith and attention to God and his only son, Jesus Christ. "I delight to do thy will, O my God: yea, thy law is within my heart," (Ps. 41:8). Sift, my dear sister, then consume.

Shawn Evans Mitchell

Cooking Terms

BAKE—To cook food, covered or uncovered, in an oven

BASTE—To moisten foods during cooking to add flavor and prevent drying

BEAT—To whipp or stir ingredients until smooth out

BLACKENED—A dish charred over heavy heat, usually with Cajun spices

BLANCH—To loosen skins from foods, usually by dipping foods in boiling water

BLEND—Combining two or more ingredients until smooth

BOIL—To cook food in a pot of liquid mixture at a high temperature

BRAISE—Cooking meat slowly on the stove in a small amount of liquid mixture

BREAD—To coat food with bread crumbs

BRINE—Salt water solution

BROIL—To cook food below direct, dry heat

BROWN—To cook cubed, sliced, or ground meat, usually by frying, until brown in color and close to thouroughly cooked

BUTTERFLY—To splitt foods through the middle without total division, often done with shrimp or chicken

CANDIED—Food cooked in a syrup base

CARVE—To cut or slice cooked meat into pieces for serving

CHILL—To cool a dish below room temperature, usually in a refrigerator

CHOP—To cut foods into small pieces

COAT—To cover foods with crumbs, flour, or batter

CREAM—To beat ingredients, usually one dry and one moist, to a light, fluffy consistency

CRIMP—To pinch or press together two edges of dough, pasta, pastry by using your fingers, a crimper, or a fork

CRUSH—to smash a seasoning to sprinkle over food

CUBE—To cut into cube-shaped pieces

CURDLE—To cause semisolid pieces of protein to form in a liquid dairy product, most often milk or cream

DE-GLAZE—To lift drippings and flavor from a skillet that has been used to cook meat by adding liquid to the pan and simmering

DIP—To put food into a wet mixture to coat

DISSOLVE—To mix solid food into a liquid food until none of the solid remains

DRAWN—Melted, as in butter

DREDGE—To coat a food with a dry mixture

DRESS—To put dressing on salad ingredients and toss together

DUST—To sprinkle a food with a dry ingredient

EMULSION—Two liquids that don't dissolve into one another.

FLAKE—To break a food into small, flat pieces

FLUTE—To make a decorative pattern in the edges of a food

FOLD—To mix ingredients by using a spatula and, with a gentle motion, lift from the bottom, up one side, and over the top in a "folding" motion; rotate bowl 1/4 turn and repeat until ingredients are mixed

FRY—To cook food in hot cooking oil: can either be done in a frying pan or by immersion in oil in a "deep" fryer

GARNISH—Decorative additions to a finished dish to make the food visually appealing

GIBLETS—Internal organs of poultry cooked and added to foods as seasoning

GLAZE—A thin and glossy coating on food

GRATE—To rub food across a rough surface to make small pieces

GREASE—To put a thin layer of butter, margarine, or shortening to a baking utensil

GRIND—To process food into small pieces using a grinder or processor with metal teeth

JUICE—To squeeze the natural juice out of a fruit

JULIENNE—To cut foods into toothpick-sized strips

KNEAD—To press and fold dough with your hands

MARBLE—To swirl one food into another

MARINADE—A seasoned liquid food is soaked in for a while to add flavor

MASH—To repeatedly pound a solid food with a tool until it becomes a smooth mixture

Cooking Terms continued on pg. 180

MELT—To heat a solid until it becomes a liquid

MINCE—To cut a food into very tiny pieces, smaller than chop or dice

MIX—To stir or beat ingredients together to make one mixture

MOISTEN—To add liquid to a dry food to make it damp

MULL—To heating a beverage slowly with spices

PAN-BROIL—To cook food in a skillet without added fat

PARE—To cut the peel off of a fruit or vegetable using a small knife

PARTIALLY SET—To chill a mixture until it gels

PECTIN—Natural substances in fruits used to make jelly

PEEL—To remove the peel off of fruit or vegetable using your hands

PIPE—Using a bag filled with a food such as icing to decorate another food

PIT—To remove the seed from fruit

PLUMP—To soak fruit in a liquid

POACH—To cooking a food by simmering in a liquid

POUND—To strike a food with a heavy utensil to tenderize it

PRECOOK—To cook the food before adding it to the recipe

PREHEAT—To heat the oven to the required cooking temperature before placing the food in it.

PROCESS—The act of canning food to preserve it

PROOF—Allowing a yeast dough to rise before baking

PURÉE—To process a solid food into a heavy paste

RECONSTITUTE—To bring a concentrated food to its original strength by adding water

REDUCE—To turn down the cooking temperature on the stove or oven

RIND—The peel of a fruit such as an orange or watermelon, or the act of removing it

ROAST—To cook a food uncovered over dry heat

ROUX—A thick, brown mixture made by cooking flour and fat

SAUTÉ—To cook food in a skillet with a little oil in order to brown it

SCALD—To heat a liquid above the boiling point

SCORE—To cut grooves through a food to tenderize it

SCRAPE—To rub the outer layer off of a food with a sharp utensil

SEAR—To brown a larger piece of meat on all sides to seal in the juices

SECTION—To divide a citrus fruit into pieces

SHRED—To pushing food across a blunt object or tear apart with your hands to form long tiny pieces

SHUCK—To remove shells from seafood or husks from corn

SIEVE—To separate food into fine particles

SIFT—To remove lumps from a dry food by shaking through a meshed utensil

SIMMER—To allow a food to cook in liquid over a low heat, but not let it boil

SKIM—To remove the gelling fat from the surface of a cooling liquid

SLICE—To cut smaller strip pieces from a whole piece

SNIP—To cut using shears

STEAM—To cook food in a vapor

STEEP—To soak tea in hot water to release flavor

STEW—To cook food in liquid for a long time until tender

STIR—To mix ingredients using a spoon

STIR-FRY—To cook food in a hot oiled wok

STOCK—The liquid from cooked meat for other cooking

TOAST—To heating until outside is a golden brown

TOSS—To mix foods by gently picking them up and dropping them with utensils

WEEPING—Separating liquid out of the solid food

WHIP—To beat a food lightly at a high speed to increase its volume by adding air

ZEST—Gratings from the outer portion of a citrus fruit used to season food

Weights and Measures

1 pound	=	454	grams
1 ounce	=	28	grams
1 quart	=	1	liter
1 cup	=	240	milliters
1 tablespoon	=	15	milliliters
1 teaspoon	=	5	milliliters
4 quarts	=	1	gallon
2 pints	=	1	quart
4 cups	=	1	quart
2 cups	=	1	pint
1 cup	=	½	pint
1 cup	=	8	fluid ounces
1 tablespoon	=	½	fluid ounce
16 tablespoon	=	1	cup
12 tablespoons	=	¾	cup
10⅔ tablespoons	=	⅔	cup
8 tablespoons	=	½	cup
5⅓ tablespoons	=	⅓	cup
4 tablespoons	=	¼	cup
3 teaspoons	=	1	tablespoon

Biography

Chandra Dixon is a member of Colgate-Palmolive's Customer Service and Logistics Management team. She is a graduate of Auburn University, where she received a Bachelor of Science Degree in Business Administration with a focus on Transportation and Logistics. She has worked as a professional in the Transportation/Logistics industry for almost 10 years and has been employed by companies such as ABF Freight System, Inc. and Wal-Mart Stores, Inc. She has contributed to the Women of Color Devotional Bible and the Wisdom and grace Devotional Bible. Chandra lives in the Greater Atlanta area with her husband, Don Dixon and their two children.

Jennifer Keitt is the founder & host of TODAY'S BLACK WOMAN RADIO SHOW, which reaches over 300,000 women weekly. She is also author of the book, The Power Of Being A Real Woman. She has earned honors for her contributions to women globally as producer and host of the her radio program. She is also President of Today's Black Woman Corporation, a non-profit organization offering education, empowerment, information and encouragement through conferences, seminars, the Today's Black Woman Chamber of Commerce and the Today's Black Woman Foundation. She has contributed to the Women of Color Devotional Bible and the Wisdom and grace Devotional Bible. She lives with her husband and their four children in Atlanta.

Linda Peavy is Associate Publisher and Director of Marketing of Judson Press in Valley Forge, PA. She holds an undergraduate degree and M.B.A. from the University of Akron, Akron, Ohio. Her work has appeared in The Book of Daily Prayer, 2001. Also, she has contributed to the Women of Color Devotional Bible

Priscilla Shirer is a Graduate of University of Houston with a degree in Communications and a Graduate of Dallas Theological Seminary with a Master degree in Biblical Studies. She is a conference speaker for major corporations and Christian audiences across the United States. She is author of "A Jewel In His Crown" and regularly published monthly articles. She is also a host of television and radio programs in Chicago, San Francisco and Dallas on CBS and other networks. Priscilla is the daughter of pastor, speaker and well-known author, Dr. Tony Evans. She and her husband Jerry live in Dallas, Texas, with their son.

Montrie Rucker Adams is a freelance writer, a director of publications, the owner of a creative marketing, research and consulting company, and volunteer for many community-based organizations. She served for ten years as editor-in-chief of Kaleidoscope, a magazine that highlights African American achievement in the Northeast Ohio. She has contributed to the Women of Color Devotional Bible.

Jeanette Taylor, is the Director of Operations for New Life Corporations, Mega Corp., and New Life Fellowship Center of Charlotte. She also serves a Business Manager for Rev. John P. Kee, pastor and artist and is an active member of the New Life Community Choir. She is a partaker of New Life Fellowship, Charlotte, N.C. were she works with the Youth and Women's Ministries and is one of the directors of The New Divine Destiny Choir.

Dina Andrews is a record company executive, artist manager, television producer, writer, and president and CEO of her own production, management and consulting firm. In addition to her role as president and CEO of Knew Beginnings Entertainment, she is the

entertainment consultant and executive producer for Axiom Entertainment, a record label owned by the New Covenant Church. She has contributed to the Women of Color Devotional Bible.

Karen Waddles is Assistant to the Publisher at Moody Press in Chicago, IL. She is the wife of Rev. George W. Waddles, Sr., pastor of the Zion Hill Baptist Church of Chicago, IL and Dean of the National Baptist Congress of Christian Education. Also, she has contributed to the Women of Color Devotional Bible. They are the proud parents of four children and five grandchildren

Michele Clark Jenkins has been a creative and business executive in the entertainment industry for 25 years. She was Director of Business Affairs for HBO, President of the BET/Tim Reid Production company and General Manager for the Estate of Dr. Martin Luther King, Jr. She was writer and editor of "The Children of Color Storybook Bible" and now develops Christian and historical properties for book, TV and film, as well as consulting for several multi-media companies. Michele, a graduate of Princeton University and New York Law School lives in Marietta, Georgia and is married to Kym Jenkins. They have three daughters.

Jessica H. Love is an inspiring writer born in Birmingham, Alabama, but raised in Columbus, Ohio. She is a graduate of Ohio University, and received a Bachelor's degree in Sociology/Criminology. She has remained remain in the investigatory field for the past 15 years. She has contributed to the Women of Color Devotional Bible. She and her husband James R. Love, have one son, James II.

Veraunda Jackson, is a former prosecuting attorney who witnessed

firsthand that people were overwhelmed and frustrated. She is a motivational speaker and author of, "Everything Has A Price!" She is the president of EHAP Inc. in Orlando, Florida.

Shawn Evans Mitchell, a veteran newspaper journalist, is on faculty in the Department of Mass Media Arts at Clark Atlanta University. She is an active member of her church, Saint Philip African Methodist Episcopalian, where she serves as a class leader and member of the Stewardess Board. She has contributed to the Women of Color Devotional Bible. Shawn also is a freelance writer and editor, and a member of Delta Sigma Theta Sorority, Inc. Shawn resides in Stone Mountain, Ga. with her husband William and their daughter.

Stephanie Perry Moore is the President of Soul Publishing, Inc. She is the author of the Payton Skky series, the Laurel Shadrach series, FLAME, and A LOVA LIKE NO OTHA. She is the Editor of the Women of Color Cookbook, the Men of Color Study Bible, and the Wisdom and Grace Bible for Young Women of Color, the Strength and Honor Bible for Young Men of Color, and the Women of Color Devotional Bible. Mrs. Moore lives in the greater Atlanta area with her husband, Derrick, and their two young daughters.

Taiwanna Brown-Bolds, MD is a physician in Internal Medicine in the Greater Atlanta Area. She attended medical school at Morehouse School of Medicine in Atlanta, GA; and residency at Medical College of Georgia in Augusta, GA. She is married to Bryant Bolds; and has two children.

Robin M. Dial is a native of Bessemer, Alabama. Robin is the President of Planting seeds ministry and co Author of Children Planting Seeds Daily Devotionals. Robin is a kindergarten teacher at Greenforest/McCaleb Christian Academic Center. She has contributed to the Women of Color Devotional Bible. Robin is married to Rev. Steven Dial Sr., the minister of Youth and students at the Greenforest Community Baptist Church in Decatur, GA where they are members. Robin is the mother of two sons and guardian of her niece.

Vanessa Salami is the owner of Midnight Joy ™ where she does full time writing and motivational speaking. She is the author of A HEART OF A GIRL IS GOD'S BUSINESS. Also, she has contributed to the Women of Color Devotional Bible and the Wisdom and grace Devotional Bible. She lives in the greater Atlanta area with her husband and their two daughters.

Monique Headley is a graduate from the University of Notre Dame with a B.A. in Government and Minor in Spanish. She is the writer of the "LaBelle!" children's book series, plays cello and loves to travel almost as much as she loves to eat good food. Currently, Monique is the Executive at Verity Records, in New York. She has contributed to the Women of Color Devotional Bible and the Wisdom and grace Devotional Bible.

Tajuana TJ Butler is a writer, poet, and public speaker who lectures on sisterhood at colleges around the country. Her published works are Hand-me-down Heartache, Sorority Sisters, and The Desires of A Woman: Poems Celebrating Womanhood. She lives in Los Angeles where she is working on a new novel.

Denise Stinson is a well-known literary agent and President of Walk Worthy Press, a Christian publishing company. She lives in the greater Detroit area.

Cathy Johnson writes and illustrates children books, and various graphic design products. She works as an illustrator for Hallmark Greeting Cards Inc. She has contributed to the Women of Color Devotional Bible. She lives in Kansas City Missouri with her son.

Portia George, formerly served as marketing sales representative for Judson Press. She has been active in Christian education for more than twenty-five years. She is the founder of "Kingdom Kids"; a program designed to help children of all ages in their journey to know Christ. The sole proprietor of PG Enterprises, the author of four African-American Christian children's books, now available on CD-ROM. Contributing author for Judson Press and Nia Publishing. Is the Director of the American Baptist Speakers Program for the American Baptist Churches USA, Valley Forge, PA. Also, she has contributed to the Women of Color Devotional Bible and the Wisdom and grace Devotional Bible. She is the wife of Dr. William Gary George. They have one son.

Jamell Meeks is a native Chicagoan and works in the communication field. She challenges women to discover and fulfill God's purpose for their lives and to become Godly influences in their homes, workplaces, communities and beyond. Under her leadership, many have fulfilled these Kingdom goals with the Women of Influence program. She has contributed to the Women of Color Devotional Bible and the Wisdom and Grace Devotional Bible. Also, she is the wife of Reverend James T. Meeks, Pastor of Salem Baptist Church of Chicago, and a mother of four.

Evangelist Marlow Shields-Talton is a nationally sought after evangelist,

public & motivational speaker. Her ministry "Divine Appointment" has been a defining part of an upcoming book release "Fragmented Pieces" and a new conference which will be held in her home city of Dallas Texas. She is the Sales Executive & Supervisor in the Sales & Marketing Division, for the world-renowned T.D. Jakes Ministries. She has contributed to the Women of Color Devotional Bible and the Wisdom and Grace Devotional Bible.

Marjorie L. Kimbrough, author, educator, is a Phi Beta Kappa graduate of the University of California and the Interdenominational Theological Center. She worked in corporate America for 28 years and taught in college for 10 years. A frequent lecturer for business, academic and religious organizations, she has published articles on business and religious subjects, has written meditations for world wide magazines, has taught on video tape, and has published five books, Accept No Limitations, Beyond Limitations, She Is Worthy, Everyday Miracles, and Stories Between the Testaments. She was also a contributing author to 365 More Meditations for Women, 365 Meditations for Mothers of Teens, and the soon to be published 365 Meditations for Families. She was the 1991 Georgia Author of the Year in the area of Non Fiction. Also, she has contributed to the Women of Color Study Bible, the Women of Color Devotional Bible and the Wisdom and Grace Devotional Bible. She is married to Rev. Walter L. Kimbrough and is the mother of two adult sons.

Otilia Taylor-Tanner is a native New Yorker. She works in the fashion industry. She is a member of Memorial Baptist Church in Harlem New York and is a part of the Pastor's Aid ministry. She and her husband have five children.

Denise Stinson is a "seeker" and president of Walk Worth Press, a Christian publishing company.

Jeanette Taylor is the Director of Operations for New Life Corporations, Mega Corp., and New Life Fellowship Center of Charlotte. She also serves as business manager for Rev. John P. Kee and is an active member of the New Life Community Choir. She is a partaker of New Life Fellowship, Charlotte, North Carolina, where she works with the youth and women's ministries and is one of the directors of The New Divine Destiny Choir.

Otilia Taylor-Tanner has spent 15 years on New York's fashion avenue and met her husband while working overseas. They have 5 children. Currently she works freelance on projects in the garment district and enjoys spending time with her children. She likes to cook, travel, and read, and is a member of the Memorial Baptist Church in Harlem, New York.

Karen Waddles is Assistant to the Publisher at Moody Press in Chicago, IL. She is the wife of Rev. George W. Waddles, Sr., pastor of the Zion Hill Baptist Church of Chicago, IL, and Dean of the National Baptist Congress of Christian Education. They are the proud parents of four children and five grandchildren.

Delores Warren has been in the food service industry for 18 years and a pastry chef for those three years. Her specialty for the past two years has been wedding and specialty cakes, dessert creations, and pastry consulting. She also does in-home consulting and dessert preparations. She is the mother of four daughters who range in age from 4 to 16 years old.

Index

ham steak   Neely's   food Network
                        4/10 @ 8:20am

onions   3 slices of bacon (fried)
carrots   " Memphis Morsels "show
garlic

swiss chard - roll then chop
                cut stem like
chick peas (16oz) celery (keep in)
                        soup
red pepper   NOT LIKE
   flakes   greens!
   chicken stock
Saute
      dice tomatoes